DAN-58   DANTES SUBJECT STANDARDIZED TESTS (DSST)

This is your
PASSBOOK for...

Ethics in America

Test Preparation Study Guide
Questions & Answers

COPYRIGHT NOTICE

This book is SOLELY intended for, is sold ONLY to, and its use is RESTRICTED to individual, bona fide applicants or candidates who qualify by virtue of having seriously filed applications for appropriate license, certificate, professional and/or promotional advancement, higher school matriculation, scholarship, or other legitimate requirements of education and/or governmental authorities.

This book is NOT intended for use, class instruction, tutoring, training, duplication, copying, reprinting, excerption, or adaptation, etc., by:

1) Other publishers
2) Proprietors and/or Instructors of "Coaching" and/or Preparatory Courses
3) Personnel and/or Training Divisions of commercial, industrial, and governmental organizations
4) Schools, colleges, or universities and/or their departments and staffs, including teachers and other personnel
5) Testing Agencies or Bureaus
6) Study groups which seek by the purchase of a single volume to copy and/or duplicate and/or adapt this material for use by the group as a whole without having purchased individual volumes for each of the members of the group
7) Et al.

Such persons would be in violation of appropriate Federal and State statutes.

PROVISION OF LICENSING AGREEMENTS – Recognized educational, commercial, industrial, and governmental institutions and organizations, and others legitimately engaged in educational pursuits, including training, testing, and measurement activities, may address request for a licensing agreement to the copyright owners, who will determine whether, and under what conditions, including fees and charges, the materials in this book may be used them. In other words, a licensing facility exists for the legitimate use of the material in this book on other than an individual basis. However, it is asseverated and affirmed here that the material in this book CANNOT be used without the receipt of the express permission of such a licensing agreement from the Publishers. Inquiries re licensing should be addressed to the company, attention rights and permissions department.

All rights reserved, including the right of reproduction in whole or in part, in any form or by any means, electronic or mechanical, including photocopying, recording, or by any information storage and retrieval system, without permission in writing from the Publisher.

Copyright © 2024 by
National Learning Corporation

212 Michael Drive, Syosset, NY 11791
(516) 921-8888 • www.passbooks.com
E-mail: info@passbooks.com

PUBLISHED IN THE UNITED STATES OF AMERICA

PASSBOOK® SERIES

THE *PASSBOOK® SERIES* has been created to prepare applicants and candidates for the ultimate academic battlefield – the examination room.

At some time in our lives, each and every one of us may be required to take an examination – for validation, matriculation, admission, qualification, registration, certification, or licensure.

Based on the assumption that every applicant or candidate has met the basic formal educational standards, has taken the required number of courses, and read the necessary texts, the *PASSBOOK® SERIES* furnishes the one special preparation which may assure passing with confidence, instead of failing with insecurity. Examination questions – together with answers – are furnished as the basic vehicle for study so that the mysteries of the examination and its compounding difficulties may be eliminated or diminished by a sure method.

This book is meant to help you pass your examination provided that you qualify and are serious in your objective.

The entire field is reviewed through the huge store of content information which is succinctly presented through a provocative and challenging approach – the question-and-answer method.

A climate of success is established by furnishing the correct answers at the end of each test.

You soon learn to recognize types of questions, forms of questions, and patterns of questioning. You may even begin to anticipate expected outcomes.

You perceive that many questions are repeated or adapted so that you can gain acute insights, which may enable you to score many sure points.

You learn how to confront new questions, or types of questions, and to attack them confidently and work out the correct answers.

You note objectives and emphases, and recognize pitfalls and dangers, so that you may make positive educational adjustments.

Moreover, you are kept fully informed in relation to new concepts, methods, practices, and directions in the field.

You discover that you are actually taking the examination all the time: you are preparing for the examination by "taking" an examination, not by reading extraneous and/or supererogatory textbooks.

In short, this PASSBOOK®, used directedly, should be an important factor in helping you to pass your test.

NONTRADITIONAL EDUCATION

Students returning to school as adults bring more varied experience to their studies than do the teenagers who begin college shortly after graduating from high school. As a result, there are numerous programs for students with nontraditional learning curves. Hundreds of colleges and universities grant degrees to people who cannot attend classes at a regular campus or have already learned what the college is supposed to teach.

You can earn nontraditional education credits in many ways:
- Passing standardized exams
- Demonstrating knowledge gained through experience
- Completing campus-based coursework, and
- Taking courses off campus

Some methods of assessing learning for credit are objective, such as standardized tests. Others are more subjective, such as a review of life experiences.

With some help from four hypothetical characters – Alice, Vin, Lynette, and Jorge – this article describes nontraditional ways of earning educational credit. It begins by describing programs in which you can earn a high school diploma without spending 4 years in a classroom. The college picture is more complicated, so it is presented in two parts: one on gaining credit for what you know through course work or experience, and a second on college degree programs. The final section lists resources for locating more information.

Earning High School Credit

People who were prevented from finishing high school as teenagers have several options if they want to do so as adults. Some major cities have back-to-school programs that allow adults to attend high school classes with current students. But the more practical alternatives for most adults are to take the General Educational Development (GED) tests or to earn a high school diploma by demonstrating their skills or taking correspondence classes.

Of course, these options do not match the experience of staying in high school and graduating with one's friends. But they are viable alternatives for adult learners committed to meeting and, often, continuing their educational goals.

GED Program

Alice quit high school her sophomore year and took a job to help support herself, her younger brother, and their newly widowed mother. Now an adult, she wants to earn her high school diploma – and then go on to college. Because her job as head cook and her family responsibilities keep her busy during the day, she plans to get a high school equivalency diploma. She will study for, and take, the GED tests. Every year, about half a million adults earn their high school credentials this way. A GED diploma is accepted in lieu of a high school one by more than 90 percent of employers, colleges, and universities, so it is a good choice for someone like Alice.

The GED testing program is sponsored by the American Council on Education and State and local education departments. It consists of examinations in five subject areas: Writing, science, mathematics, social studies, and literature and the arts. The tests also measure skills such as analytical ability, problem solving, reading comprehension, and ability to understand and apply information. Most of the questions are multiple choice; the writing test includes an essay section on a topic of general interest.

Eligibility rules for taking the exams vary, but some states require that you must be at least 18. Tests are given in English, Spanish, and French. In addition to standard print, versions in large print, Braille, and audiocassette are also available. Total time allotted for the tests is 7 1/2 hours.

The GED tests are not easy. About one-fourth of those who complete the exams every year do not pass. Passing scores are established by administering the tests to a sample of graduating high school seniors. The minimum standard score is set so that about one-third of graduating seniors would not pass the tests if they took them.

Because of the difficulty of the tests, people need to prepare themselves to take them. Often, they start by taking the Official GED Practice Tests, usually available through a local adult education center. Centers are listed in your phone book's blue pages under "Adult Education," "Continuing Education," or "GED." Adult education centers also have information about GED preparation classes and self-study materials. Classes are generally arranged to accommodate adults' work schedules. National Learning Corporation publishes several study guides that aim to thoroughly prepare test-takers for the GED.

School districts, colleges, adult education centers, and community organizations have information about GED testing schedules and practice tests. For more information, contact them, your nearest GED testing center, or:

GED Testing Service
One Dupont Circle, NW, Suite 250
Washington, DC 20036-1163
1(800) 62-MY GED (626-9433)
(202) 939-9490

Skills Demonstration

Adults who have acquired high school level skills through experience might be eligible for the National External Diploma Program. This alternative to the GED does not involve any direct instruction. Instead, adults seeking a high school diploma must demonstrate mastery of 65 competencies in 8 general areas: Communication; computation; occupational preparedness; and self, social, consumer, scientific, and technological awareness.

Mastery is shown through the completion of the tasks. For example, a participant could prove competency in computation by measuring a room for carpeting, figuring out the amount of carpet needed, and computing the cost.

Before being accepted for the program, adults undergo an evaluation. Tests taken at one of the program's offices measure reading, writing, and mathematics abilities. A take-home segment includes a self-assessment of current skills, an individual skill evaluation, and an occupational interest and aptitude test.

Adults accepted for the program have weekly meetings with an assessor. At the meeting, the assessor reviews the participant's work from the previous week. If the task has not been completed properly, the assessor explains the mistake. Participants continue to correct their errors until they master each competency. A high school diploma is awarded upon proven mastery of all 65 competencies.

Fourteen States and the District of Columbia now offer the External Diploma Program. For more information, contact:

External Diploma Program
One Dupont Circle, NW, Suite 250
Washington, DC 20036-1193
(202) 939-9475

Correspondence and Distance Study

Vin dropped out of high school during his junior year because his family's frequent moves made it difficult for him to continue his studies. He promised himself at the time he dropped out that he would someday finish the courses needed for his diploma. For people like Vin, who prefer to earn a traditional diploma in a nontraditional way, there are about a dozen accredited courses of study for earning a high school diploma by correspondence, or distance study. The programs are either privately run, affiliated with a university, or administered by a State education department.

Distance study diploma programs have no residency requirements, allowing students to continue their studies from almost any location. Depending on the course of study, students need not be enrolled full time and usually have more flexible schedules for finishing their work. Selection of courses ranges from vo-tech to college prep, and some programs place different emphasis on the types of diplomas offered. University affiliated schools, for example, allow qualified students to take college courses along with their high school ones. Students can then apply the college credits toward a degree at that university or transfer them to another institution.

Taking courses by distance study is often more challenging and time consuming than attending classes, especially for adults who have other obligations. Success depends on each student's motivation. Students usually do reading assignments on their own. Written exercises, which they complete and send to an instructor for grading, supplement their reading material.

A list of some accredited high schools that offer diplomas by distance study is available free from the Distance Education and Training Council, formerly known as the National Home Study Council. Request the "DETC Directory of Accredited Institutions" from:

The Distance Education and Training Council
1601 18th Street, NW.
Washington, DC 20009-2529
(202) 234-5100

Some publications profiling nontraditional college programs include addresses and descriptions of several high school correspondence ones. See the Resources section at the end of this article for more information.

Getting College Credit For What You Know

Adults can receive college credit for prior coursework, by passing examinations, and documenting experiential learning. With help from a college advisor, nontraditional students should assess their skills, establish their educational goals, and determine the number of college credits they might be eligible for.

Even before you meet with a college advisor, you should collect all your school and training records. Then, make a list of all knowledge and abilities acquired through experience, no matter how irrelevant they seem to your chosen field. Next, determine your educational goals: What specific field do you wish to study? What kind of a degree do you want? Finally, determine how your past work fits into the field of study. Later on, you will evaluate educational programs to find one that's right for you.

People who have complex educational or experiential learning histories might want to have their learning evaluated by the Regents Credit Bank. The Credit Bank, operated by Regents College of the University of the State of New York, allows people to consolidate credits earned through college, experience, or other methods. Special assessments are available for Regents College enrollees whose knowledge in a specific field cannot be adequately evaluated by standardized exams. For more information, contact the Regents Credit Bank at:

Regents College
7 Columbia Circle
Albany, NY 12203-5159
(518) 464-8500

Credit For Prior College Coursework

When Lynette was in college during the 1970s, she attended several different schools and took a variety of courses. She did well in some classes and poorly in others. Now that she is a successful business owner and has more focus, Lynette thinks she should forget about her previous coursework and start from scratch. Instead, she should start from where she is.

Lynette should have all her transcripts sent to the colleges or universities of her choice and let an admissions officer determine which classes are applicable toward a degree. A few credits here and there may not seem like much, but they add up. Even if the subjects do not seem relevant to any major, they might be counted as elective credits toward a degree. And comparing the cost of transcripts with the cost of college courses, it makes sense to spend a few dollars per transcript for a chance to save hundreds, and perhaps thousands, of dollars in books and tuition.

Rules for transferring credits apply to all prior coursework at accredited colleges and universities, whether done on campus or off. Courses completed off campus, often called extended learning, include those available to students through independent study and correspondence. Many schools have extended learning programs; Brigham Young University, for example, offers more than 300 courses through its Department of Independent Study. One type of extended learning is distance learning, a form of correspondence study by technological means such as television, video and audio, CD-ROM, electronic mail, and computer tutorials. See the Resources section at the end of this article for more information about publications available from the National University Continuing Education Association.

Any previously earned college credits should be considered for transfer, no matter what the subject or the grade received. Many schools do not accept the transfer of courses graded below a C or ones taken more than a designated number of years ago. Some colleges and universities also have limits on the number of credits that can be transferred and applied toward a degree. But not all do. For example, Thomas Edison State College, New Jersey's State college for adults, accepts the transfer of all 120 hours of credit required for a baccalaureate degree – provided all the credits are transferred from regionally accredited schools, no more than 80 are at the junior college level, and the student's grades overall and in the field of study average out to C.

To assign credit for prior coursework, most schools require original transcripts. This means you must complete a form or send a written, signed request to have your transcripts released directly to a college or university. Once you have chosen the schools you want to apply to, contact the schools you attended before. Find out how much each transcript costs, and ask them to send your transcripts to the ones you are applying to. Write a letter that includes your name (and names used during attendance, if different) and dates of attendance, along with the names and addresses of the schools to which your transcripts should be sent. Include payment and mail to the registrar at the schools you have attended. The registrar's office will process your request and send an official transcript of your coursework to the colleges or universities you have designated.

Credit For Noncollege Courses

Colleges and universities are not the only ones that offer classes. Volunteer organizations and employers often provide formal training worth college credit. The American Council on Education has two programs that assess thousands of specific courses and make recommendations on the amount of college credit they are worth. Colleges and universities accept the recommendations or use them as guidelines.

One program evaluates educational courses sponsored by government agencies, business and industry, labor unions, and professional and voluntary organizations. It is the Program on Noncollegiate Sponsored Instruction (PONSI). Some of the training seminars Alice has participated in covered topics such as food preparation, kitchen safety, and nutrition. Although she has not yet earned her GED, Alice can earn college credit because of her completion of these formal job-training seminars. The number of credits each seminar is worth does not hinge on Alice's current eligibility for college enrollment.

The other program evaluates courses offered by the Army, Navy, Air Force, Marines, Coast Guard, and Department of Defense. It is the Military Evaluations Program. Jorge has never attended college, but the engineering technology classes he completed as part of his military training are worth college credit. And as an Army veteran, Jorge is eligible for a service that takes the evaluations one step further. The Army/American Council on Education Registry Transcript System (AARTS) will provide Jorge with an individualized transcript of American Council on Education credit recommendations for all courses he completed, the military occupational specialties (MOS's) he held, and examinations he passed while in the Army. All Army and National Guard enlisted personnel and veterans who enlisted after October 1981 are eligible for the transcript. Similar services are being considered by the Navy and Marine Corps.

To obtain a free transcript, see your Army Education Center for a 5454R transcript request form. Include your name, Social Security number, basic active service date, and complete address where you want the transcript sent. Mail your request to:

AARTS Operations Center
415 McPherson Ave.
Fort Leavenworth, KS 66027-1373

Recommendations for PONSI are published in *The National Guide to Educational Credit for Training Programs;* military program recommendations are in *The Guide to the Evaluation of Educational Experiences in the Armed Forces.* See the Resources section at the end of this article for more information about these publications.

Former military personnel who took a foreign language course through the Defense Language Institute may request course transcripts by sending their name, Social Security number, course title, duration of the course, and graduation date to:

Commandant, Defense Language Institute
Attn: ATFL-DAA-AR
Transcripts
Presidio of Monterey
Monterey, CA 93944-5006

Not all of Jorge's and Alice's courses have been assessed by the American Council on Education. Training courses that have no Council credit recommendation should still be assessed by an advisor at the schools they want to attend. Course descriptions, class notes, test scores, and other documentation may be helpful for comparing training courses to their college equivalents. An oral examination or other demonstration of competency might also be required.

There is no guarantee you will receive all the credits you are seeking – but you certainly won't if you make no attempt.

Credit By Examination

Standardized tests are the best-known method of receiving college credit without taking courses. These exams are often taken by high school students seeking advanced placement for college, but they are also available to adult learners. Testing programs and colleges and universities offer exams in a number of subjects. Two U.S. Government institutes have foreign language exams for employees that also may be worth college credit.

It is important to understand that receiving a passing score on these exams does not mean you get college credit automatically. Each school determines which test results it will accept, minimum scores required, how scores are converted for credit, and the amount of credit, if any, to be assigned. Most colleges and universities accept the American Council on Education credit recommendations, published every other year in the 250-page *Guide to Educational Credit by Examination*. For more information, contact:

The American Council on Education
Credit by Examination Program
One Dupont Circle, Suite 250
Washington, DC 20036-1193
(202) 939-9434

Testing programs:

You might know some of the five national testing programs by their acronyms or initials: CLEP, ACT PEP: RCE, DANTES, AP, and NOCTI. (The meanings of these initialisms are explained below.) There is some overlap among programs; for example, four of them have introductory accounting exams. Since you will not be awarded credit more than once for a specific subject, you should carefully evaluate each program for the subject exams you wish to take. And before taking an exam, make sure you will be awarded credit by the college or university you plan to attend.

CLEP (College-Level Examination Program), administered by the College Board, is the most widely accepted of the national testing programs; more than 2,800 accredited schools award credit for passing exam scores. Each test covers material taught in basic undergraduate courses. There are five general exams – English composition, humanities, college mathematics, natural sciences, and social sciences and history – and many subject exams. Most exams are entirely multiple-choice, but English composition exams may include an essay section. For more information, contact:

    CLEP
    P.O. Box 6600
    Princeton, NJ 08541-6600
    (609) 771-7865

ACT PEP: RCE (American College Testing Proficiency Exam Program: Regents College Examinations) tests are given in 38 subjects within arts and sciences, business, education, and nursing. Each exam is recommended for either lower- or upper-level credit. Exams contain either objective or extended response questions, and are graded according to a standard score, letter grade, or pass/fail. Fees vary, depending on the subject and type of exam. For more information or to request free study guides, contact:

    ACT PEP: Regents College Examinations
    P.O. Box 4014
    Iowa City, IA 52243
    (319) 337-1387
    (New York State residents must contact Regents College directly.)

DANTES (Defense Activity for Nontraditional Education Support) standardized tests are developed by the Educational Testing Service for the Department of Defense. Originally administered only to military personnel, the exams have been available to the public since 1983. About 50 subject tests cover business, mathematics, social science, physical science, humanities, foreign languages, and applied technology. Most of the tests consist entirely of multiple-choice questions. Schools determine their own administering fees and testing schedules. For more information or to request free study sheets, contact:

    DANTES Program Office
    Mail Stop 31-X
    Educational Testing Service
    Princeton, NJ 08541
    1(800) 257-9484

The AP (Advanced Placement) Program is a cooperative effort between secondary schools and colleges and universities. AP exams are developed each year by committees of college and high school faculty appointed by the College Board and assisted by consultants from the Educational Testing Service. Subjects include arts and languages, natural sciences, computer science, social sciences, history, and mathematics. Most tests are 2 or 3 hours long and include both multiple-choice and essay questions. AP courses are available to help students prepare for exams, which are offered in the spring. For more information about the Advanced Placement Program, contact:

    Advanced Placement Services
    P.O. Box 6671
    Princeton, NJ 08541-6671
    (609) 771-7300

NOCTI (National Occupational Competency Testing Institute) assessments are designed for people like Alice, who have vocational-technical skills that cannot be evaluated by other tests. NOCTI assesses competency at two levels: Student/job ready and teacher/experienced worker. Standardized evaluations are available for occupations such as auto-body repair, electronics, mechanical drafting, quantity food preparation, and upholstering. The tests consist of multiple-choice questions and a performance component. Other services include workshops, customized assessments, and pre-testing. For more information, contact:

NOCTI
500 N. Bronson Ave.
Ferris State University
Big Rapids, MI 49307
(616) 796-4699

Colleges and universities:

Many colleges and universities have credit-by-exam programs, through which students earn credit by passing a comprehensive exam for a course offered by the institution. Among the most widely recognized are the programs at Ohio University, the University of North Carolina, Thomas Edison State College, and New York University.

Ohio University offers about 150 examinations for credit. In addition, you may sometimes arrange to take special examinations in non-laboratory courses offered at Ohio University. To take a test for credit, you must enroll in the course. If you plan to transfer the credit earned, you also need written permission from an official at your school. Books and study materials are available, for a cost, through the university. Exams must be taken within 6 months of the enrollment date; most last 3 hours. You may arrange to take the exam off campus if you do not live near the university.

Ohio University is on the quarter-hour system; most courses are worth 4 quarter hours, the equivalent of 3 semester hours. For more information, contact:

Independent Study
Tupper Hall 302
Ohio University
Athens, OH 45701-2979
1(800) 444-2910
(614) 593-2910

The University of North Carolina offers a credit-by-examination option for 140 independent study (correspondence) courses in foreign languages, humanities, social sciences, mathematics, business administration, education, electrical and computer engineering, health administration, and natural sciences. To take an exam, you must request and receive approval from both the course instructor and the independent studies department. Exams must be taken within six months of enrollment, and you may register for no more than two at a time. If you are not near the University's Chapel Hill campus, you may take your exam under supervision at an accredited college, university, community college, or technical institute. For more information, contact:

Independent Studies
CB #1020, The Friday Center
UNC-Chapel Hill
Chapel Hill, NC 27599-1020
1(800) 862-5669 / (919) 962-1134

The Thomas Edison College Examination Program offers more than 50 exams in liberal arts, business, and professional areas. Thomas Edison State College administers tests twice a month in Trenton, New Jersey; however, students may arrange to take their tests with a proctor at any accredited American college or university or U.S. military base. Most of the tests are multiple choice; some also include short answer or essay questions. Time limits range from 90 minutes to 4 hours, depending on the exam. For more information, contact:

Thomas Edison State College
TECEP, Office of Testing and Assessment
101 W. State Street
Trenton, NJ 08608-1176
(609) 633-2844

New York University's Foreign Language Program offers proficiency exams in more than 40 languages, from Albanian to Yiddish. Two exams are available in each language: The 12-point test is equivalent to 4 undergraduate semesters, and the 16-point exam may lead to upper level credit. The tests are given at the university's Foreign Language Department throughout the year.

Proof of foreign language proficiency does not guarantee college credit. Some colleges and universities accept transcripts only for languages commonly taught, such as French and Spanish. Nontraditional programs are more likely than traditional ones to grant credit for proficiency in other languages.

For an informational brochure and registration form for NYU's foreign language proficiency exams, contact:

New York University
Foreign Language Department
48 Cooper Square, Room 107
New York, NY 10003
(212) 998-7030

Government institutes:

The Defense Language Institute and Foreign Service Institute administer foreign language proficiency exams for personnel stationed abroad. Usually, the tests are given at the end of intensive language courses or upon completion of service overseas. But some people – like Jorge, who knows Spanish – speak another language fluently and may be allowed to take a proficiency exam in that language before completing their tour of duty. Contact one of the offices listed below to obtain transcripts of those scores. Proof of proficiency does not guarantee college credit, however, as discussed above.

To request score reports from the Defense Language Institute for Defense Language Proficiency Tests, send your name, Social Security number, language for which you were tested, and, most importantly, when and where you took the exam to:

Commandant, Defense Language Institute
Attn: ATFL-ES-T
DLPT Score Report Request
Presidio of Monterey
Monterey, CA 93944-5006

To request transcripts of scores for Foreign Service Institute exams, send your name, Social Security number, language for which you were tested, and dates or year of exams to:

Foreign Service Institute
Arlington Hall
4020 Arlington Boulevard
Rosslyn, VA 22204-1500
Attn: Testing Office (Send your request to the attention of the testing office of the foreign language in which you were tested)

Credit For Experience

Experiential learning credit may be given for knowledge gained through job responsibilities, personal hobbies, volunteer opportunities, homemaking, and other experiences. Colleges and universities base credit awards on the knowledge you have attained, not for the experience alone. In addition, the knowledge must be college level; not just any learning will do. Throwing horseshoes as a hobby is not likely to be worth college credit. But if you've done research on how and where the sport originated, visited blacksmiths, organized tournaments, and written a column for a trade journal – well, that's a horseshoe of a different color.

Adults attempting to get credit for their experience should be forewarned: Having your experience evaluated for college credit is time-consuming, tedious work – not an easy shortcut for people who want quick-fix college credits. And not all experience, no matter how valuable, is the equivalent of college courses.

Requesting college credit for your experiential learning can be tricky. You should get assistance from a credit evaluations officer at the school you plan to attend, but you should also have a general idea of what your knowledge is worth. A common method for converting knowledge into credit is to use a college catalog. Find course titles and descriptions that match what you have learned through experience, and request the number of credits offered for those courses.

Once you know what credit to ask for, you must usually present your case in writing to officials at the college you plan to attend. The most common form of presenting experiential learning for credit is the portfolio. A portfolio is a written record of your knowledge along with a request for equivalent college credit. It includes an identification and description of the knowledge for which you are requesting credit, an explanatory essay of how the knowledge was gained and how it fits into your educational plans, documentation that you have acquired such knowledge, and a request for college credit. Required elements of a portfolio vary by schools but generally follow those guidelines.

In identifying knowledge you have gained, be specific about exactly what you have learned. For example, it is not enough for Lynette to say she runs a business. She must identify the knowledge she has gained from running it, such as personnel management, tax law, marketing strategy, and inventory review. She must also include brief descriptions about her knowledge of each to support her claims of having those skills.

The essay gives you a chance to relay something about who you are. It should address your educational goals, include relevant autobiographical details, and be well organized, neat, and convey confidence. In his essay, Jorge might first state his goal of becoming an engineer. Then he would explain why he joined the Army, where he got hands-on training and experience in developing and servicing electronic equipment.

This, he would say, led to his hobby of creating remote-controlled model cars, of which he has built 20. His conclusion would highlight his accomplishments and tie them to his desire to become an electronic engineer.

Documentation is evidence that you've learned what you claim to have learned. You can show proof of knowledge in a variety of ways, including audio or video recordings, letters from current or former employers describing your specific duties and job performance, blueprints, photographs or artwork, and transcripts of certifying exams for professional licenses and certification – such as Alice's certification from the American Culinary Federation. Although documentation can take many forms, written proof alone is not always enough. If it is impossible to document your knowledge in writing, find out if your experiential learning can be assessed through supplemental oral exams by a faculty expert.

Earning a College Degree

Nontraditional students often have work, family, and financial obligations that prevent them from quitting their jobs to attend school full time. Can they still meet their educational goals? Yes.

More than 150 accredited colleges and universities have nontraditional bachelor's degree programs that require students to spend little or no time on campus; over 300 others have nontraditional campus-based degree programs. Some of those schools, as well as most junior and community colleges, offer associate's degrees nontraditionally. Each school with a nontraditional course of study determines its own rules for awarding credit for prior coursework, exams, or experience, as discussed previously. Most have charges on top of tuition for providing these special services.

Several publications profile nontraditional degree programs; see the Resources section at the end of this article for more information. To determine which school best fits your academic profile and educational goals, first list your criteria. Then, evaluate nontraditional programs based on their accreditation, features, residency requirements, and expenses. Once you have chosen several schools to explore further, write to them for more information. Detailed explanations of school policies should help you decide which ones you want to apply to.

Get beyond the printed word – especially the glowing words each school writes about itself. Check out the schools you are considering with higher education authorities, alumni, employers, family members, and friends. If possible, visit the campus to talk to students and instructors and sit in on a few classes, even if you will be completing most or all of your work off campus. Ask school officials questions about such things as enrollment numbers, graduation rate, faculty qualifications, and confusing details about the application process or academic policies. After you have thoroughly investigated each prospective college or university, you can make an informed decision about which is right for you.

Accreditation

Accreditation is a process colleges and universities submit to voluntarily for getting their credentials. An accredited school has been investigated and visited by teams of observers and has periodic inspections by a private accrediting agency. The initial review can take two years or more.

Regional agencies accredit entire schools, and professional agencies accredit either specialized schools or departments within schools. Although there are no national accrediting standards, not just any accreditation will do. Countless "accreditation associations" have been invented by schools, many of which have no academic programs and sell phony degrees, to accredit themselves. But 6 regional and about 80 professional accrediting associations in the United States are recognized by the U.S. Department of Education or the Commission on Recognition of Postsecondary Accreditation. When checking accreditation, these are the names to look for. For more information about accreditation and accrediting agencies, contact:

> Institutional Participation Oversight Service Accreditation and State Liaison Division
> U.S. Department of Education
> ROB 3, Room 3915
> 600 Independence Ave., SW
> Washington, DC 20202-5244
> (202) 708-7417

Because accreditation is not mandatory, lack of accreditation does not necessarily mean a school or program is bad. Some schools choose not to apply for accreditation, are in the process of applying, or have educational methods too unconventional for an accrediting association's standards. For the nontraditional student, however, earning a degree from a college or university with recognized accreditation is an especially important consideration. Although nontraditional education is becoming more widely accepted, it is not yet mainstream. Employers skeptical of a degree earned in a nontraditional manner are likely to be even less accepting of one from an unaccredited school.

Program Features

Because nontraditional students have diverse educational objectives, nontraditional schools are diverse in what they offer. Some programs are geared toward helping students organize their scattered educational credits to get a degree as quickly as possible. Others cater to those who may have specific credits or experience but need assistance in completing requirements. Whatever your educational profile, you should look for a program that works with you in obtaining your educational goals.

A few nontraditional programs have special admissions policies for adult learners like Alice, who plan to earn their GEDs but want to enroll in college in the meantime. Other features of nontraditional programs include individualized learning agreements, intensive academic counseling, cooperative learning and internship placement, and waiver of some prerequisites or other requirements – as well as college credit for prior coursework, examinations, and experiential learning, all discussed previously.

Lynette, whose primary goal is to finish her degree, wants to earn maximum credits for her business experience. She will look for programs that do not limit the number of credits awarded for equivalency exams and experiential learning. And since well-documented proof of knowledge is essential for earning experiential learning credits, Lynette should make sure the program she chooses provides assistance to students submitting a portfolio.

Jorge, on the other hand, has more credits than he needs in certain areas and is willing to forego some. To become an engineer, he must have a bachelor's degree; but because he is accustomed to hands-on learning, Jorge is interested in getting experience as he gains more technical skills. He will concentrate on finding schools with strong cooperative education, supervised fieldwork, or internship programs.

Residency Requirements

Programs are sometimes deemed nontraditional because of their residency requirements. Many people think of residency for colleges and universities in terms of tuition, with in-state students paying less than out-of-state ones. Residency also may refer to where a student lives, either on or off campus, while attending school.

But in nontraditional education, residency usually refers to how much time students must spend on campus, regardless of whether they attend classes there. In some nontraditional programs, students need not ever step foot on campus. Others require only a very short residency, such as one day or a few weeks. Many schools have standard residency requirements of several semesters but schedule classes for evenings or weekends to accommodate working adults.

Lynette, who previously took courses by independent study, prefers to earn credits by distance study. She will focus on schools that have no residency requirement. Several colleges and universities have nonresident degree completion programs for adults with some college credit. Under the direction of a faculty advisor, students devise a plan for earning their remaining credits. Methods for earning credits include independent study, distance learning, seminars, supervised fieldwork, and group study at arranged sites. Students may have to earn a certain number of credits through the degree-granting institution. But many programs allow students to take courses at accredited schools of their choice for transfer toward their degree.

Alice wants to attend lectures but has an unpredictable schedule. Her best course of action will be to seek out short residency programs that require students to attend seminars once or twice a semester. She can take courses that are televised and videotape them to watch when her schedule permits, with the seminars helping to ensure that she properly completes her coursework. Many colleges and universities with short residency requirements also permit students to earn some credits elsewhere, by whatever means the student chooses.

Some fields of study require classroom instruction. As Jorge will discover, few colleges and universities allow students to earn a bachelor's degree in engineering entirely through independent study. Nontraditional residency programs are designed to accommodate adults' daytime work schedules. Jorge should look for programs offering evening, weekend, summer, and accelerated courses.

Tuition and Other Expenses

The final decisions about which schools Alice, Jorge, and Lynette attend may hinge in large part on a single issue: Cost. And rising tuition is only part of the equation. Beginning with application fees and continuing through graduation fees, college expenses add up.

Traditional and nontraditional students have some expenses in common, such as the cost of books and other materials. Tuition might even be the same for some courses, especially for colleges and universities offering standard ones at unusual times. But for nontraditional programs, students may also pay fees for services such as credit or transcript review, evaluation, advisement, and portfolio assessment.

Students are also responsible for postage and handling or setup expenses for independent study courses, as well as for all examination and transcript fees for transferring credits. Usually, the more nontraditional the program, the more detailed the fees. Some schools charge a yearly enrollment fee rather than tuition for degree completion candidates who want their files to remain active.

Although tuition and fees might seem expensive, most educators tell you not to let money come between you and your educational goals. Talk to someone in the financial aid department of the school you plan to attend or check your library for publications about financial aid sources. The U.S. Department of Education publishes a guide to Federal aid programs such as Pell Grants, student loans, and work-study. To order the free 74-page booklet, *The Student Guide: Financial Aid from the U.S. Department of Education,* contact:

Federal Student Aid Information Center
P.O. Box 84
Washington, DC 20044
1 (800) 4FED-AID (433-3243)

Resources

Information on how to earn a high school diploma or college degree without following the usual routes is available from several organizations and in numerous publications. Information on nontraditional graduate degree programs, available for master's through doctoral level, though not discussed in this article, can usually be obtained from the same resources that detail bachelor's degree programs.

National Learning Corporation publishes study guides for all of these exams, for both general examinations and tests in specific subject areas. To order study guides, or to browse their catalog featuring more than 5,000 titles, visit NLC online at www.passbooks.com, or contact them by phone at (800) 632-8888.

Organizations

Adult learners should always contact their local school system, community college, or university to learn about programs that are readily available. The following national organizations can also supply information:

American Council on Education
One Dupont Circle
Washington, DC 20036-1193
(202) 939-9300

Within the American Council on Education, the Center for Adult Learning and Educational Credentials administers the National External Diploma Program, the GED Program, the Program on Noncollegiate Sponsored Instruction, the Credit by Examination Program, and the Military Evaluations Program.

DANTES Subject Standardized Tests

INTRODUCTION

The DANTES (Defense Activity for Non-Traditional Education Support) subject standardized tests are comprehensive college and graduate level examinations given by the Armed Forces, colleges and graduate schools as end-of-subject course evaluation final examinations or to obtain college equivalency credits in the various subject areas tested.

The DANTES Examination Program enables students to obtain college credit for what they have learned on the job, through self-study, personal interest, correspondence courses or by any other means. It is used by colleges and universities to award college credit to students who demonstrate that they know as much as students completing an equivalent college course. It is a cost-efficient, time-saving way for students to use their knowledge to accomplish their educational goals.

Most schools accept the American Council on Education (ACE) recommendations for the minimum score required and the amount of credit awarded, but not all schools do. Be sure to check the policy regarding the score level required for credit and the number of credits to be awarded.

Not all tests are accepted by all institutions. Even when a test is accepted by an institution, it may not be acceptable for every program at that institution. Before considering testing, ascertain the acceptability of a specific test for a particular course.

Colleges and universities that administer DANTES tests may administer them to any applicant – or they may administer the tests only to students registered at their institution. Decisions about who will be allowed to test are made by the school. Students should contact the test center to determine current policies and schedules for DANTES testing.

Colleges and universities authorized to administer DANTES tests usually do so throughout the calendar year. Each school sets its own fee for test administration and establishes its own testing schedule. Contact the representative at the administering school directly to make arrangements for testing.

Checklist
For Students

✓ Visit **www.getcollegecredit.com** to obtain a list of tests, fact sheets, test preparation materials, participating colleges and universities, and much more.

✓ Contact your school advisor to confirm that the DSST you selected will fit into your curriculum.

✓ Consult the ***DSST Candidate Information Bulletin*** for answers to specific questions.

✓ Contact the test site to schedule your test.

✓ Prepare for your examination by using the fact sheet as a guide.

✓ Take the test.

If you would like a score report sent to your college or university, it is a good idea to bring the four-digit code with you. You must write the DSST Test Center Code for that institution on your answer sheet at the time of testing. DSST Test Center Codes are noted in the DSST Participating Colleges and Universities listing on the Web site.

If you prefer to send a score report to an institution at a later date, there is a transcript fee of $20 for each transcript ordered.

Thomson Prometric
DSST Program
2000 Lenox Drive, Third Floor
Lawrenceville, NJ 08648

Toll-free: 877-471-9860
609-895-5011

E-mail: pnj-dsst@thomson.com

parts of this introduction excerpted for educational purposes from the official announcement ©2006 Thompson Prometric

MAKING A COLLEGE DEGREE WITHIN YOUR REACH

Today, there are many educational alternatives to the classroom—you can learn from your job, your reading, your independent study, and special interests you pursue. You may already have learned the subject matter covered by some college-level courses.

The DSST Program is a nationally recognized testing program that gives you the opportunity to receive college credit for learning acquired outside the traditional college classroom. Colleges and universities throughout the United States administer the program, developed by Thomson Prometric, year-round. Annually, over 90,000 DSSTs are administered to individuals who are interested in continuing their education. Take advantage of the DSST testing program; it speeds the educational process and provides the flexibility adults need, making earning a degree more feasible.

Since requirements differ from college to college, please check with the credit-awarding institution before taking a DSST. More than 1,800 colleges and universities currently award credit for DSSTs, and the number is growing every day. You can choose from 37 test titles in the areas of Social Science, Business, Mathematics, Applied Technology, Humanities, and Physical Science. A brief description of each examination is found on the pages that follow.

Reach Your Career Goals Through DSSTs

Use DSSTs to help you earn your degree, get a promotion, or simply demonstrate that you have college-level knowledge in subjects relevant to your work.

Save Time...

You don't have to sit through classes when you have previously acquired the knowledge or experience for most of what is being taught and can learn the rest yourself. You might be able to bypass introductory-level courses in subject areas you already know.

Save Money...

DSSTs save you money because the classes you bypass by earning credit through the DSST Program are classes you won't have to pay for on your way to earning your degree. You can use the money instead to take more advanced courses that can be more challenging and rewarding.

Improve Your Chances for Admission to College

Each college has its own admission policies; however, having passing scores for DSSTs on your transcript can provide strong evidence of how well you can perform at the college level.

Gain Confidence Performing at a College Level

Many adults returning to college find that lack of confidence is often the greatest hurdle to overcome. Passing a DSST demonstrates your ability to perform on a college level.

Make Up for Courses You May Have Missed

You may be ready to graduate from college and find that you are a few credits short of earning your degree. By using semester breaks, vacation time, or leisure time to study independently, you can prepare to take one or more DSSTs, fulfill your academic requirements, and graduate on time.

If You Cannot Attend Regularly Scheduled Classes...

If your lifestyle or responsibilities prevent you from attending regularly scheduled classes, you can earn your college degree from a college offering an external degree program. The DSST Program allows you to earn your degree by study and experience outside the traditional classroom.

Many colleges and universities offer external degree or distance learning programs. For additional information, contact the college you plan to attend or:

Center for Lifelong Learning
American Council on Education
One DuPont Circle NW, Suite 250
Washington, DC 20036
202-939-9475
www.acenet.edu
(Select "Center for Lifelong Learning" under "Programs & Services"
for more information)

Fact Sheets

For each test, there is a Fact Sheet that outlines the topics covered by each test and includes a list of sample questions, a list of recommended references of books that would be useful for review, and the number of credits awarded for a passing score as recommended by the American Council on Education (ACE). *Please note that some schools require scores that are higher than the minimum ACE-recommended passing score.* It is suggested that you check with your college or university to determine what score they require in order to earn credit. You can obtain Fact Sheets by:

- Downloading them from www.getcollegecredit.com
- E-mailing a request to pnj-dsst@thomson.com
- Completing a Candidate Publications Order Form

DSST Online Practice Tests

DSST online practice tests contain items that reflect a *partial range of difficulty* identified in the Content Outline section on each Fact Sheet. There is an online DSST Practice Test in the following categories:

- Mathematics
- Social Science
- Business
- Physical Science
- Applied Technology
- Humanities

Although the online DSST Practice Test questions do not indicate the full range of difficulty you would find in an actual DSST test, they will help you assess your knowledge level. Each online DSST Practice Test can be purchased by visiting www.getcollegecredit.com and clicking on DSST Practice Exams.

TAKING DSST EXAMINATIONS

Earning College Credit for DSST Examinations

To find out if the college of your choice awards credit for passing DSST scores, contact the admissions office or counseling and testing office. The college can also provide information on the scores required for awarding credit, the number of credit hours awarded, and any courses that can be bypassed with satisfactory scores.

It is important that you contact the institution of your choice as early as possible since credit-awarding policies differ among colleges and universities.

Where to Take DSSTs

DSSTs are administered at colleges and universities nationwide. Each location determines the frequency and scheduling of test administrations. To obtain the most current list of participating DSST colleges and universities:
- Visit and download the information from www.getcollegecredit.com
- E-mail pnj-dsst@thomson.com

Scheduling Your Examination

Please be aware that some colleges and universities provide DSST testing services to enrolled students only. After you have selected a college or university that administers DSSTs, you will need to contact them to schedule your test date.

The fee to take a DSST is $60 per test. This fee entitles you to two score reports after the test is scored. One will be sent directly to you and the other will be sent to the college or university that you designate on your answer sheet. You may pay the test fee with a certified check or U.S. money order made payable to Thomson Prometric or you may charge the test fee to your Visa, MasterCard or American Express credit card. Note: The credit card statement will reflect a charge from Thomson Prometric for all DSST examinations. *(Declined credit card charges will be assessed an additional $25 processing fee.)*

In addition, the test site may also require a test administration fee for each examination, to be paid directly to the institution. Contact the test site to determine its administration fee and payment policy.

Other Testing Arrangements

If you are unable to find a participating DSST college or university in your area, you may want to contact the testing office of a local accredited college or university to determine whether a representative from that office will agree to administer the test(s) for you.

The school's representative should then contact the DSST Program at 866-794-3497 to arrange for this administration. If you are unable to locate a test site, contact Thomson Prometric for assistance at pnj-dsst@thomson.com or 866-794-3497.

Testing Accommodations for Students with Disabilities

Thomson Prometric is committed to serving test takers with disabilities by providing services and reasonable testing accommodations as set forth in the provisions of the *Americans with Disabilities Act* (ADA). If you have a disability, as prescribed by the ADA, and require special testing services or arrangements, please contact the test administrator at the test site. You will be asked to submit to the test administrator documentation of your disability and your request for special accommodations. The test administrator will then forward your documentation along with your request for testing accommodations to Thomson Prometric for approval.

Please submit your request as far in advance of your test date as possible so that the necessary accommodations can be made. Only test takers with documented disabilities are eligible for special accommodations.

On the Day of the Examination

It is important to review this information and to have the correct identification present on the day of the examination:

- Arrive on time as a courtesy to the test administrator.
- Bring a valid form of government-issued identification that includes a current photo and your signature (acceptable documents include a driver's license, passport, state-issued identification card or military identification). *Anyone who fails to present valid identification will not be allowed to test.*
- Bring several No. 2 (soft-lead) sharpened pencils with good erasers, a watch, and a black pen if you will be writing an essay.
- Do not bring books or papers.
- Do not bring an alarm watch that beeps, a telephone, or a phone beeper into the testing room.
- The use of nonprogrammable calculators, slide rules, scratch paper and/or other materials is permitted for some of the tests.

DSST SCORING POLICIES

Your DSST examination scores are reported only to you, unless you request that they be sent elsewhere. If you want your scores sent to your college, you must provide the correct DSST code number of the school on your answer sheet at the time you take the test. See the *DSST Directory of Colleges and Universities* on the Web site www.getcollegecredit.com.

If your institution is not listed, contact Thomson Prometric at 866-794-3497 to establish a code number. (Some schools may require a student to be enrolled prior to receiving a score report.)

Receiving Your Score Report

Allow approximately four weeks after testing to receive your score report.

Calling DSST Customer Service before the required four-week score processing time has elapsed will not expedite the processing of your scores. Due to privacy and security requirements, scores will not be reported to students over the telephone under any circumstance.

Scoring of Principles of Public Speaking Speeches

The speech portion of the *Principles of Public Speaking* examination will be sent to speech raters who are faculty members at accredited colleges that currently teach or have previously taught the course. Scores for the *Principles of Public Speaking* examination are available six to eight weeks from receipt by Thomson Prometric. If you take the *Principles of Public Speaking* examination and fail (either the objective, speech portion, or both), you must follow the retesting policy waiting period of six months (180 days) before retaking the entire exam.

Essays

The essays for *Ethics in America* and *Technical Writing* are <u>optional</u> and thus are not scored by raters. The essays are forwarded to the college or university that you designate, along with your score report, for their use in determining the award of credit. <u>Before taking the *Ethics in America* or *Technical Writing* examinations, check with your college or university to determine whether the essay is required.</u>

NOTE: *Principles of Public Speaking* speech topic cassette tapes and essays are kept on file at Thomson Prometric for one year from the date of administration.

How to Get Transcripts

There is a $20 fee for each transcript you request. Payment must be in the form of a certified check, U.S. money order payable to Thomson Prometric, or credit card. Personal checks and debit cards are NOT an acceptable method of payment. One transcript may include scores for one or more examinations taken. To request a transcript, download the Transcript Order Form from www.getcollegecredit.com.

DESCRIPTION OF THE DSST EXAMINATIONS

Mathematics

- **Fundamentals of College Algebra** covers mathematical concepts such as fundamental algebraic operations; linear, absolute value; quadratic equations, inequalities, radials, exponents and logarithms, factoring polynomials and graphing. The use of a nonprogrammable, handheld calculator is permitted.

- **Principles of Statistics** tests the understanding of the various topics of statistics, both qualitatively and quantitatively, and the ability to apply statistical methods to solve a variety of problems. The topics included in this test are descriptive statistics; correlation and regression; probability; chance models and sampling and tests of significance. The use of a nonprogrammable, handheld calculator is permitted.

Social Science

- **Art of the Western World** deals with the history of art during the following periods: classical; Romanesque and Gothic; early Renaissance; high Renaissance, Baroque; rococo; neoclassicism and romanticism; realism, impressionism and post-impressionism; early twentieth century; and post-World War II.

- **Western Europe Since 1945** tests the knowledge of basic facts and terms and the understanding of concepts and principles related to the areas of the historical background of the aftermath of the Second World War and rebuilding of Europe; national political systems; issues and policies in Western European societies; European institutions and processes; and Europe's relations with the rest of the world.

- **An Introduction to the Modern Middle East** emphasizes core knowledge (including geography, Judaism, Christianity, Islam, ethnicity); nineteenth-century European impact; twentieth-century Western influences; World Wars I and II; new nations; social and cultural changes (1900-1960) and the Middle East from 1960 to present.

- **Human/Cultural Geography** includes the Earth and basic facts (coordinate systems, maps, physiography, atmosphere, soils and vegetation, water); culture and environment, spatial processes (social processes, modern economic systems, settlement patterns, political geography); and regional geography.

- **Rise and Fall of the Soviet Union** covers Russia under the Old Regime; the Revolutionary Period; New Economic Policy; Pre-war Stalinism; The Second World War; Post-war Stalinism; The Khrushchev Years; The Brezhnev Era; and reform and collapse.

- **A History of the Vietnam War** covers the history of the roots of the Vietnam War; the First Vietnam War (1946-1954); pre-war developments (1954-1963); American involvement in the Vietnam War; Tet (1968); Vietnamizing the War (1968-1973); Cambodia and Laos; peace; legacies and lessons.

- **The Civil War and Reconstruction** covers the Civil War from presecession (1861) through Reconstruction. It includes causes of the war; secession; Fort Sumter; the war in the east and in the west; major battles; the political situation; assassination of Lincoln; end of the Confederacy; and Reconstruction.

- **Foundations of Education** includes topics such as contemporary issues in education; past and current influences on education (philosophies, democratic ideals, social/economic influences); and the interrelationships between contemporary issues and influences.

- **Life-span Developmental Psychology** covers models and theories; methods of study; ethical issues; biological development; perception, learning and memory; cognition and language; social, emotional, and personality development; social behaviors, family life cycle, extrafamilial settings; singlehood and cohabitation; occupational development and retirement; adjustment to life stresses; and bereavement and loss.

- **Drug and Alcohol Abuse** includes such topics as drug use in society; classification of drugs; pharmacological principles; alcohol (types, effects of, alcoholism); general principles and use of sedative hypnotics, narcotic analgesics, stimulants, and hallucinogens; other drugs (inhalants, steroids); and prevention/treatment.

- **General Anthropology** deals with anthropology as a discipline; theoretical perspectives; physical anthropology; archaeology; social organization; economic organization; political organization; religion; and modernization and application of anthropology.

- **Introduction to Law Enforcement** includes topics such as history and professional movement of law enforcement; overview of the U.S. criminal justice system; police systems in the U.S.; police organization, management, and issues; and U.S. law and precedents.

- **Criminal Justice** deals with criminal behavior (crime in the U.S., theories of crime, types of crime); the criminal justice system (historical origins, legal foundations, due process); police; the court system (history and organization, adult court system, juvenile court, pre-trial and post-trial processes); and corrections.

- **Fundamentals of Counseling** covers historical development (significant influences and people); counselor roles and functions; the counseling relationship; and theoretical approaches to counseling.

Business
- **Principles of Finance** deals with financial statements and planning; time value of money; working capital management; valuation and characteristics; capital budgeting; cost of capital; risk and return; and international financial management. The use of a nonprogrammable, handheld calculator is permitted.

- **Principles of Financial Accounting** includes topics such as general concepts and principles; accounting cycle and classification; transaction analysis; accruals and deferrals; cash and internal control; current accounts; long- and short-term liabilities; capital stock; and financial statements. The use of a nonprogrammable, handheld calculator is permitted.

- **Human Resource Management** covers general employment issues; job analysis; training and development; performance appraisals; compensation issues; security issues; personnel legislation and regulation; labor relations and current issues; an overview of the Human Resource Management Field; Human Resource Planning; Staffing; training and development; compensation issues; safety and health; employee rights and discipline; employment law; labor relations and current issues and trends.

- **Organizational Behavior** deals with the study of organizational behavior (scientific approaches, research designs, data collection methods); individual processes and characteristics; interpersonal and group processes and characteristics; organizational processes and characteristics; and change and development processes.

- **Principles of Supervision** deals with the roles and responsibilities of the supervisor; management functions (planning, organization and staffing, directing at the supervisory level); and other topics (legal issues, stress management, union environments, quality concerns).

- **Business Law II** covers topics such as sales of goods; debtor and creditor relations; business organizations; property; and commercial paper.

- **Introduction to Computing** includes topics such as history and technological generations; hardware/software; applications to information technology; program development; data management; communications and connectivity; and computing and society. The use of a nonprogrammable, handheld calculator is permitted.

- **Management Information Systems** covers systems theory, analysis and design of systems, hardware and software; database management; telecommunications; management of the MIS functional area and informational support.

- **Introduction to Business** deals with economic issues affecting business; international business; government and business; forms of business ownership; small business, entrepreneurship and franchise; management process; human resource management; production and operations; marketing management; financial management; risk management and insurance; and management and information systems.

- **Money and Banking** covers the role and kinds of money; commercial banks and other financial intermediaries; central banking and the Federal Reserve system; money and macroeconomics activity; monetary policy in the U.S.; and the international monetary system.

- **Personal Finance** includes topics such as financial goals and values; budgeting; credit and debt; major purchases; taxes; insurance; investments; and retirement and estate planning. The use of auxiliary materials, such as calculators and slide rules, is NOT permitted.

- **Business Mathematics** deals with basic operations with integers, fractions, and decimals; round numbers; ratios; averages; business graphs; simple interest; compound interest and annuities; net pay and deductions; discounts and markups; depreciation and net worth; corporate securities; distribution of ownership; and stock and asset turnover.

Physical Science
• **Astronomy** covers the history of astronomy, celestial mechanics; celestial systems; astronomical instruments; the solar system; nature and evolution; the galaxy; the universe; determining astronomical distances; and life in the universe.

• **Here's to Your Health** covers mental health and behavior; human development and relationships; substance abuse; fitness and nutrition; risk factors, disease, and disease prevention; and safety, consumer awareness, and environmental concerns.

• **Environment and Humanity** deals with topics such as ecological concepts (ecosystems, global ecology, food chains and webs); environmental impacts; environmental management and conservation; and political processes and the future.

• **Principles of Physical Science I** includes physics: Newton's Laws of Motion; energy and momentum; thermodynamics; wave and optics; electricity and magnetism; chemistry: properties of matter; atomic theory and structure; and chemical reactions.

• **Physical Geology** covers Earth materials; igneous, sedimentary, and metamorphic rocks; surface processes (weathering, groundwater, glaciers, oceanic systems, deserts and winds, hydrologic cycle); internal Earth processes; and applications (mineral and energy resources, environmental geology).

Applied Technology
• **Technical Writing** covers topics such as theory and practice of technical writing; purpose, content, and organizational patterns of common types of technical documents; elements of various technical reports; and technical editing. Students have the option to write a short essay on one of the technical topics provided. Thomson Prometric will not score the essay; however, for determining the award of credit, a copy of the essay will be forwarded to the college or university you've designated along with the score report or transcript.

Humanities
• **Ethics in America** deals with ethical traditions (Greek views, Biblical traditions, moral law, consequential ethics, feminist ethics); ethical analysis of issues arising in interpersonal and personal-societal relationships and in professional and occupational roles; and relationships between ethical traditions and the ethical analysis of situations. Students have the option to write an essay to analyze a morally problematic situation in terms of issues relevant to a decision and arguments for alternative positions. Thomson Prometric will not score the essay; however, for determining the award of credit, a copy of the essay will be forwarded to the college or university you've designated along with the score report or transcript.

• **Introduction to World Religions** covers topics such as dimensions and approaches to religion; primal religions; Hinduism; Buddhism; Confucianism; Taoism; Judaism; Christianity; and Islam.

• **Principles of Public Speaking** consists of two parts: Part One consists of multiple-choice questions covering considerations of Principles of Public Speaking; audience analysis; purposes of speeches; structure/organization; content/supporting materials; research; language and style; delivery; communication apprehension; listening and feedback; and criticism and evaluation. Part Two requires the student to record an impromptu persuasive speech that will be scored.

FREQUENTLY ASKED QUESTIONS ABOUT DSSTs

In order to pass the test, must I study from one of the recommended references?

The recommended references are a listing of books that were being used as textbooks in college courses of the same or similar title at the time the test was developed. Appropriate textbooks for study are not limited to those listed in the fact sheet. If you wish to obtain study resources to prepare for the examination, you may reference either the current edition of the listed titles or textbooks currently used at a local college or university for the same class title. It is recommended that you reference more than one textbook on the topics outlined in the fact sheet. You should begin by checking textbook content against the content outline included on the front page of the DSST fact sheet before selecting textbooks that cover the text content from which to study. Textbooks may be found at the campus bookstore of a local college or university offering a course on the subject.

Is there a penalty for guessing on the tests?

There is no penalty for guessing on DSSTs, so you should mark an answer for each question.

How much time will I have to complete the test?

Many DSSTs can be completed within 90 minutes; however, additional time can be allowed if necessary.

What should I do if I find a test question irregularity?

Continue testing and then report the irregularity to the test administrator after the test. This may be done by asking that the test administrator note the irregularity on the Supervisor's Irregularity Report or you can write to Thomson Prometric, DSST Program, 2000 Lenox Drive, Third Floor, Lawrenceville, NJ 08648, and indicate the form and question number(s) or circumstances as well as your name and address.

When will I receive my score report?

Allow approximately four weeks from the date of testing to receive your score report. Allow six to eight weeks to receive a score report for the *Principles of Public Speaking* examination.

Will my test scores be released without my permission?

Your test score will not be released to anyone other than the school you designate on your answer sheet unless you write to us and ask us to send a transcript elsewhere. Instructions about how to do this can be found on your score report. Your scores may be used for research purposes, but individual scores are never made public nor are individuals identified if research findings are made public.

If I do not achieve a passing score on the test, how long must I wait until I can take the test again?

If you do not receive a score on the test that will enable you to obtain credit for the course, you may take the test again after six months (180 days). Please do not attempt to take the test before six months (180 days) have passed because you will receive a score report marked *invalid* and your test fee will not be refunded.

Can my test scores be canceled?

The test administrator is required to report any irregularities to Thomson Prometric. <u>The consequence of bringing unauthorized materials into the testing room, or giving or receiving help, will be the forfeiture of your test fee and the invalidation of test scores.</u> The DSST Program reserves the right to cancel scores and not issue score reports in such situations.

What can I do if I feel that my test scores were not accurately reported?

Thomson Prometric recognizes the extreme importance of test results to candidates and has a multi-step quality-control procedure to help ensure that reported scores are accurate. If you have reason to believe that your score(s) were not accurately reported, you may request to have your answer sheet reviewed and hand scored.

The fees for this service are:
- $20 fee if requested within six months of the test date
- $30 fee if requested more than six months from the test date
- $30 fee if a re-evaluation of the *Principles of Public Speaking* speech is requested

The fee for this service can be paid by credit card or by certified check or U.S. money order payable to Thomson Prometric. Submit your request for score verification along with the appropriate fee or credit card information (credit card number and expiration date) to Thomson Prometric, DSST Program, 2000 Lenox Drive, Third Floor, Lawrenceville, NJ 08648. Include your full name, the test title, the date you took the test, and your Social Security number. Candidates will be notified if a scoring discrepancy is discovered within four weeks of receipt of the request.

What does ACE recommendation mean?

The ACE recommendation is the minimum passing score recommended by the American Council on Education for any given test. It is equivalent to the average score of students in the DSST norming sample who received a grade of C for the course. Some schools require a score higher than the ACE recommendation.

Who is NLC?

National Learning Corporation (NLC) has been successfully preparing candidates for 40 years for over 5,000 exams. NLC publishes Passbook® study guides to help candidates prepare for all DANTES and CLEP exams and almost every other type of exam from high school through adult career.

Go to our website — www.passbooks.com — or call (800) 632-8888 for information about ordering our Passbooks.

To get detailed information on the DSST program and DSST preparation materials, visit www.getcollegecredit.com.

If you are interested in taking the DSST exams, call 877-471-9860 or e-mail pnj-dsst@thomson.com.

HOW TO TAKE A TEST

You have studied long, hard and conscientiously.

With your official admission card in hand, and your heart pounding, you have been admitted to the examination room.

You note that there are several hundred other applicants in the examination room waiting to take the same test.

They all appear to be equally well prepared.

You know that nothing but your best effort will suffice. The "moment of truth" is at hand: you now have to demonstrate objectively, in writing, your knowledge of content and your understanding of subject matter.

You are fighting the most important battle of your life—to pass and/or score high on an examination which will determine your career and provide the economic basis for your livelihood.

What extra, special things should you know and should you do in taking the examination?

I. YOU MUST PASS AN EXAMINATION

A. WHAT EVERY CANDIDATE SHOULD KNOW
Examination applicants often ask us for help in preparing for the written test. What can I study in advance? What kinds of questions will be asked? How will the test be given? How will the papers be graded?

B. HOW ARE EXAMS DEVELOPED?
Examinations are carefully written by trained technicians who are specialists in the field known as "psychological measurement," in consultation with recognized authorities in the field of work that the test will cover. These experts recommend the subject matter areas or skills to be tested; only those knowledges or skills important to your success on the job are included. The most reliable books and source materials available are used as references. Together, the experts and technicians judge the difficulty level of the questions.
Test technicians know how to phrase questions so that the problem is clearly stated. Their ethics do not permit "trick" or "catch" questions. Questions may have been tried out on sample groups, or subjected to statistical analysis, to determine their usefulness.
Written tests are often used in combination with performance tests, ratings of training and experience, and oral interviews. All of these measures combine to form the best-known means of finding the right person for the right job.

II. HOW TO PASS THE WRITTEN TEST

A. BASIC STEPS

1) Study the announcement

How, then, can you know what subjects to study? Our best answer is: "Learn as much as possible about the class of positions for which you've applied." The exam will test the knowledge, skills and abilities needed to do the work.

Your most valuable source of information about the position you want is the official exam announcement. This announcement lists the training and experience qualifications. Check these standards and apply only if you come reasonably close to meeting them. Many jurisdictions preview the written test in the exam announcement by including a section called "Knowledge and Abilities Required," "Scope of the Examination," or some similar heading. Here you will find out specifically what fields will be tested.

2) Choose appropriate study materials

If the position for which you are applying is technical or advanced, you will read more advanced, specialized material. If you are already familiar with the basic principles of your field, elementary textbooks would waste your time. Concentrate on advanced textbooks and technical periodicals. Think through the concepts and review difficult problems in your field.

These are all general sources. You can get more ideas on your own initiative, following these leads. For example, training manuals and publications of the government agency which employs workers in your field can be useful, particularly for technical and professional positions. A letter or visit to the government department involved may result in more specific study suggestions, and certainly will provide you with a more definite idea of the exact nature of the position you are seeking.

3) Study this book!

III. KINDS OF TESTS

Tests are used for purposes other than measuring knowledge and ability to perform specified duties. For some positions, it is equally important to test ability to make adjustments to new situations or to profit from training. In others, basic mental abilities not dependent on information are essential. Questions which test these things may not appear as pertinent to the duties of the position as those which test for knowledge and information. Yet they are often highly important parts of a fair examination. For very general questions, it is almost impossible to help you direct your study efforts. What we can do is to point out some of the more common of these general abilities needed in public service positions and describe some typical questions.

1) General information

Broad, general information has been found useful for predicting job success in some kinds of work. This is tested in a variety of ways, from vocabulary lists to questions about current events. Basic background in some field of work, such as sociology or economics, may be sampled in a group of questions. Often these are principles which have become familiar to most persons through exposure rather than through formal training. It is difficult to advise you how to study for these questions; being alert to the world around you is our best suggestion.

2) Verbal ability

An example of an ability needed in many positions is verbal or language ability. Verbal ability is, in brief, the ability to use and understand words. Vocabulary and grammar tests are typical measures of this ability. Reading comprehension or paragraph interpretation questions are common in many kinds of civil service tests. You are given a paragraph of written material and asked to find its central meaning.

IV. KINDS OF QUESTIONS

1. Multiple-choice Questions

Most popular of the short-answer questions is the "multiple choice" or "best answer" question. It can be used, for example, to test for factual knowledge, ability to solve problems or judgment in meeting situations found at work.

A multiple-choice question is normally one of three types:
- It can begin with an incomplete statement followed by several possible endings. You are to find the one ending which best completes the statement, although some of the others may not be entirely wrong.
- It can also be a complete statement in the form of a question which is answered by choosing one of the statements listed.
- It can be in the form of a problem – again you select the best answer.

Here is an example of a multiple-choice question with a discussion which should give you some clues as to the method for choosing the right answer:

When an employee has a complaint about his assignment, the action which will best help him overcome his difficulty is to
- A. discuss his difficulty with his coworkers
- B. take the problem to the head of the organization
- C. take the problem to the person who gave him the assignment
- D. say nothing to anyone about his complaint

In answering this question, you should study each of the choices to find which is best. Consider choice "A" – Certainly an employee may discuss his complaint with fellow employees, but no change or improvement can result, and the complaint remains unresolved. Choice "B" is a poor choice since the head of the organization probably does not know what assignment you have been given, and taking your problem to him is known as "going over the head" of the supervisor. The supervisor, or person who made the assignment, is the person who can clarify it or correct any injustice. Choice "C" is, therefore, correct. To say nothing, as in choice "D," is unwise. Supervisors have and interest in knowing the problems employees are facing, and the employee is seeking a solution to his problem.

2. True/False

3. Matching Questions

Matching an answer from a column of choices within another column.

V. RECORDING YOUR ANSWERS

Computer terminals are used more and more today for many different kinds of exams.

For an examination with very few applicants, you may be told to record your answers in the test booklet itself. Separate answer sheets are much more common. If this separate answer sheet is to be scored by machine – and this is often the case – it is highly important that you mark your answers correctly in order to get credit.

VI. BEFORE THE TEST

YOUR PHYSICAL CONDITION IS IMPORTANT

If you are not well, you can't do your best work on tests. If you are half asleep, you can't do your best either. Here are some tips:

1) Get about the same amount of sleep you usually get. Don't stay up all night before the test, either partying or worrying—DON'T DO IT!
2) If you wear glasses, be sure to wear them when you go to take the test. This goes for hearing aids, too.
3) If you have any physical problems that may keep you from doing your best, be sure to tell the person giving the test. If you are sick or in poor health, you relay cannot do your best on any test. You can always come back and take the test some other time.

Common sense will help you find procedures to follow to get ready for an examination. Too many of us, however, overlook these sensible measures. Indeed, nervousness and fatigue have been found to be the most serious reasons why applicants fail to do their best on civil service tests. Here is a list of reminders:

- Begin your preparation early – Don't wait until the last minute to go scurrying around for books and materials or to find out what the position is all about.
- Prepare continuously – An hour a night for a week is better than an all-night cram session. This has been definitely established. What is more, a night a week for a month will return better dividends than crowding your study into a shorter period of time.
- Locate the place of the exam – You have been sent a notice telling you when and where to report for the examination. If the location is in a different town or otherwise unfamiliar to you, it would be well to inquire the best route and learn something about the building.
- Relax the night before the test – Allow your mind to rest. Do not study at all that night. Plan some mild recreation or diversion; then go to bed early and get a good night's sleep.
- Get up early enough to make a leisurely trip to the place for the test – This way unforeseen events, traffic snarls, unfamiliar buildings, etc. will not upset you.
- Dress comfortably – A written test is not a fashion show. You will be known by number and not by name, so wear something comfortable.
- Leave excess paraphernalia at home – Shopping bags and odd bundles will get in your way. You need bring only the items mentioned in the official notice you received; usually everything you need is provided. Do not bring reference books to the exam. They will only confuse those last minutes and be taken away from you when in the test room.

- Arrive somewhat ahead of time – If because of transportation schedules you must get there very early, bring a newspaper or magazine to take your mind off yourself while waiting.
- Locate the examination room – When you have found the proper room, you will be directed to the seat or part of the room where you will sit. Sometimes you are given a sheet of instructions to read while you are waiting. Do not fill out any forms until you are told to do so; just read them and be prepared.
- Relax and prepare to listen to the instructions
- If you have any physical problem that may keep you from doing your best, be sure to tell the test administrator. If you are sick or in poor health, you really cannot do your best on the exam. You can come back and take the test some other time.

VII. AT THE TEST

The day of the test is here and you have the test booklet in your hand. The temptation to get going is very strong. Caution! There is more to success than knowing the right answers. You must know how to identify your papers and understand variations in the type of short-answer question used in this particular examination. Follow these suggestions for maximum results from your efforts:

1) Cooperate with the monitor

The test administrator has a duty to create a situation in which you can be as much at ease as possible. He will give instructions, tell you when to begin, check to see that you are marking your answer sheet correctly, and so on. He is not there to guard you, although he will see that your competitors do not take unfair advantage. He wants to help you do your best.

2) Listen to all instructions

Don't jump the gun! Wait until you understand all directions. In most civil service tests you get more time than you need to answer the questions. So don't be in a hurry. Read each word of instructions until you clearly understand the meaning. Study the examples, listen to all announcements and follow directions. Ask questions if you do not understand what to do.

3) Identify your papers

Civil service exams are usually identified by number only. You will be assigned a number; you must not put your name on your test papers. Be sure to copy your number correctly. Since more than one exam may be given, copy your exact examination title.

4) Plan your time

Unless you are told that a test is a "speed" or "rate of work" test, speed itself is usually not important. Time enough to answer all the questions will be provided, but this does not mean that you have all day. An overall time limit has been set. Divide the total time (in minutes) by the number of questions to determine the approximate time you have for each question.

5) Do not linger over difficult questions

If you come across a difficult question, mark it with a paper clip (useful to have along) and come back to it when you have been through the booklet. One caution if you do this – be sure to skip a number on your answer sheet as well. Check often to be sure that you have not lost your place and that you are marking in the row numbered the same as the question you are answering.

6) Read the questions
   Be sure you know what the question asks! Many capable people are unsuccessful because they failed to read the questions correctly.

7) Answer all questions
   Unless you have been instructed that a penalty will be deducted for incorrect answers, it is better to guess than to omit a question.

8) Speed tests
   It is often better NOT to guess on speed tests. It has been found that on timed tests people are tempted to spend the last few seconds before time is called in marking answers at random – without even reading them – in the hope of picking up a few extra points. To discourage this practice, the instructions may warn you that your score will be "corrected" for guessing. That is, a penalty will be applied. The incorrect answers will be deducted from the correct ones, or some other penalty formula will be used.

9) Review your answers
   If you finish before time is called, go back to the questions you guessed or omitted to give them further thought. Review other answers if you have time.

10) Return your test materials
    If you are ready to leave before others have finished or time is called, take ALL your materials to the monitor and leave quietly. Never take any test material with you. The monitor can discover whose papers are not complete, and taking a test booklet may be grounds for disqualification.

VIII. EXAMINATION TECHNIQUES

1) Read the general instructions carefully. These are usually printed on the first page of the exam booklet. As a rule, these instructions refer to the timing of the examination; the fact that you should not start work until the signal and must stop work at a signal, etc. If there are any special instructions, such as a choice of questions to be answered, make sure that you note this instruction carefully.

2) When you are ready to start work on the examination, that is as soon as the signal has been given, read the instructions to each question booklet, underline any key words or phrases, such as least, best, outline, describe and the like. In this way you will tend to answer as requested rather than discover on reviewing your paper that you listed without describing, that you selected the worst choice rather than the best choice, etc.

3) If the examination is of the objective or multiple-choice type – that is, each question will also give a series of possible answers: A, B, C or D, and you are called upon to select the best answer and write the letter next to that answer on your answer paper – it is advisable to start answering each question in turn. There may be anywhere from 50 to 100 such questions in the three or four hours allotted and you can see how much time would be taken if you read through all the questions before beginning to answer any. Furthermore, if you

come across a question or group of questions which you know would be difficult to answer, it would undoubtedly affect your handling of all the other questions.

4) If the examination is of the essay type and contains but a few questions, it is a moot point as to whether you should read all the questions before starting to answer any one. Of course, if you are given a choice – say five out of seven and the like – then it is essential to read all the questions so you can eliminate the two that are most difficult. If, however, you are asked to answer all the questions, there may be danger in trying to answer the easiest one first because you may find that you will spend too much time on it. The best technique is to answer the first question, then proceed to the second, etc.

5) Time your answers. Before the exam begins, write down the time it started, then add the time allowed for the examination and write down the time it must be completed, then divide the time available somewhat as follows:
   - If 3-1/2 hours are allowed, that would be 210 minutes. If you have 80 objective-type questions, that would be an average of 2-1/2 minutes per question. Allow yourself no more than 2 minutes per question, or a total of 160 minutes, which will permit about 50 minutes to review.
   - If for the time allotment of 210 minutes there are 7 essay questions to answer, that would average about 30 minutes a question. Give yourself only 25 minutes per question so that you have about 35 minutes to review.

6) The most important instruction is to read each question and make sure you know what is wanted. The second most important instruction is to time yourself properly so that you answer every question. The third most important instruction is to answer every question. Guess if you have to but include something for each question. Remember that you will receive no credit for a blank and will probably receive some credit if you write something in answer to an essay question. If you guess a letter – say "B" for a multiple-choice question – you may have guessed right. If you leave a blank as an answer to a multiple-choice question, the examiners may respect your feelings but it will not add a point to your score. Some exams may penalize you for wrong answers, so in such cases only, you may not want to guess unless you have some basis for your answer.

7) Suggestions
   a. Objective-type questions
      1. Examine the question booklet for proper sequence of pages and questions
      2. Read all instructions carefully
      3. Skip any question which seems too difficult; return to it after all other questions have been answered
      4. Apportion your time properly; do not spend too much time on any single question or group of questions
      5. Note and underline key words – all, most, fewest, least, best, worst, same, opposite, etc.
      6. Pay particular attention to negatives
      7. Note unusual option, e.g., unduly long, short, complex, different or similar in content to the body of the question
      8. Observe the use of "hedging" words – probably, may, most likely, etc.

9. Make sure that your answer is put next to the same number as the question
10. Do not second-guess unless you have good reason to believe the second answer is definitely more correct
11. Cross out original answer if you decide another answer is more accurate; do not erase until you are ready to hand your paper in
12. Answer all questions; guess unless instructed otherwise
13. Leave time for review

b. Essay questions
1. Read each question carefully
2. Determine exactly what is wanted. Underline key words or phrases.
3. Decide on outline or paragraph answer
4. Include many different points and elements unless asked to develop any one or two points or elements
5. Show impartiality by giving pros and cons unless directed to select one side only
6. Make and write down any assumptions you find necessary to answer the questions
7. Watch your English, grammar, punctuation and choice of words
8. Time your answers; don't crowd material

8) Answering the essay question

Most essay questions can be answered by framing the specific response around several key words or ideas. Here are a few such key words or ideas:

M's: manpower, materials, methods, money, management
P's: purpose, program, policy, plan, procedure, practice, problems, pitfalls, personnel, public relations

a. Six basic steps in handling problems:
1. Preliminary plan and background development
2. Collect information, data and facts
3. Analyze and interpret information, data and facts
4. Analyze and develop solutions as well as make recommendations
5. Prepare report and sell recommendations
6. Install recommendations and follow up effectiveness

b. Pitfalls to avoid
1. Taking things for granted – A statement of the situation does not necessarily imply that each of the elements is necessarily true; for example, a complaint may be invalid and biased so that all that can be taken for granted is that a complaint has been registered
2. Considering only one side of a situation – Wherever possible, indicate several alternatives and then point out the reasons you selected the best one
3. Failing to indicate follow up – Whenever your answer indicates action on your part, make certain that you will take proper follow-up action to see how successful your recommendations, procedures or actions turn out to be
4. Taking too long in answering any single question – Remember to time your answers properly

EXAMINATION SECTION

EXAMINATION SECTION
TEST 1

DIRECTIONS: Each question or incomplete statement is followed by several suggested answers or completions. Select the one that BEST answers the question or completes the statement. *PRINT THE LETTER OF THE CORRECT ANSWER IN THE SPACE AT THE RIGHT.*

1. A *dogmatic* person is someone who
    I. listens to others' arguments and then decides
    II. listens to others' arguments but never decides
    III. never listens to others' arguments
    IV. offers reasons for his view
    V. never offers reasons for his view
   The CORRECT answer is:

   A. I only
   B. II only
   C. III, IV
   D. IV only
   E. III, V

   1._____

2. An *eclectic* philosophy is one that
    I. draws upon a variety of theories for its conclusion
    II. relies upon a fundamental component for its basis
    III. speculates freely and relies upon nothing
    IV. combines several elements
    V. has a unitary simplicity
   The CORRECT answer is:

   A. I, IV
   B. I, V
   C. II, III
   D. II, III, IV
   E. III, IV, V

   2._____

3. The psychological theory which has provided a rationale for capitalism is

   A. altruism
   B. egoism
   C. relativism
   D. Freudianism
   E. none of the above

   3._____

4. An EQUIVOCATION is a logical fallacy caused by

   A. false assumptions
   B. invalid inferences
   C. ambiguous statements
   D. listeners jumping to conclusions
   E. all of the above

   4._____

5. The study of ESCHATOLOGY concerns _____ things.

   A. first
   B. last
   C. all
   D. God's
   E. human

   5._____

6. The ancient Greek root of the English word "ethics" meant

   6._____

1

A. life B. virtue
C. love D. duty
E. custom

7. EUPHEMISMS are words that
   I. don't mean anything
   II. can mean just about anything
   III. substitute for other, more concrete, words
   IV. substitute for other, more vague, words
   V. should be used sparingly, if at all
   The CORRECT answer is:

   A. I, II B. II *only*
   C. II, III, V D. III, V
   E. IV, V

8. Some existentialist philosophers are
   I. Hume
   II. Marx
   III. Kierkegaard
   IV. Sartre
   V. Camus
   The CORRECT answer is:

   A. I, II B. I, II, III
   C. I, III, IV D. II, IV, V
   E. III, IV, V

9. EXISTENTIALISM maintains that
   I. I am, therefore I think
   II. no one knows anything
   III. life is absurd
   IV. suicide is noble
   V. we don't choose to be born
   The CORRECT answer is:

   A. I, III, IV, V B. II, III
   C. II, IV, V D. III, IV, V
   E. all of the above

10. Facts are those things *contrasted* with
    I. a priori truths
    II. logical axioms
    III. necessary truths
    IV. falsehoods
    V. speculations
    The CORRECT answer is:

    A. I *only* B. I, II
    C. I, II, III D. II, III, V
    E. III, IV, V

11. FATALISM is the view that
    I. the Fates know what is in store for us
    II. you will not die until your time is come
    III. everything that happens was meant to happen
    IV. nothing that happens was meant to happen
    V. no one knows what it means
    The CORRECT answer is:

    A. I, II
    B. II, III
    C. II, IV
    D. II, IV, V
    E. III, V

12. Philosophers who believed in the "Greatest Happiness Principle" were
    I. Plato
    II. Bentham
    III. Mill
    IV. Rousseau
    V. Epicurus
    The CORRECT answer is:

    A. I, II, III, V
    B. I, III, IV, V
    C. II, III, IV
    D. II, III, IV, V
    E. all of the above

13. *Deontological* ethics emphasizes the concept(s) of
    I. justice
    II. rights
    III. duty
    IV. goodness
    V. virtue
    The CORRECT answer is:

    A. I *only*
    B. II *only*
    C. II, III
    D. II, III, IV
    E. III, IV, V

14. *Teleological* ethics emphasizes

    A. justice
    B. rights
    C. duty
    D. goodness
    E. virtue

15. Among philosophers emphasizing *hedonism* are
    I. Plato
    II. Epicurus
    III. Kant
    IV. Hobbes
    V. Bentham
    The CORRECT answer is:

    A. I, II
    B. I, III
    C. II, III, IV
    D. II, IV, V
    E. II, V

16. Hegel's philosophy was a form of
    I. materialism
    II. idealism
    III. dialecticism
    IV. absolutism
    V. opportunism
    The CORRECT answer is:

    A. I, II
    B. II, III
    C. II, III, IV
    D. II, IV
    E. III, IV, V

17. Philosophers who were *heavily* influenced by Hegel were
    I. Aristotle
    II. Plotinus
    III. Marx
    IV. Fichte
    V. Kierkegaard
    The CORRECT answer is:

    A. I, III
    B. II, III
    C. II, III, IV
    D. III, IV
    E. III, V

18. The view that reality changes constantly and that no one can "step into the same river twice" is attributed to

    A. Plato
    B. Aristotle
    C. Plotinus
    D. Heraclitus
    E. Democritus

19. The first historians are *commonly* believed to be
    I. Marcus Aurelius
    II. Aristotle
    III. Goebbels
    IV. Thucydides
    V. Herodotus
    The CORRECT answer is:

    A. I, II
    B. I, II, III
    C. II, III
    D. II, IV, V
    E. IV, V

20. The author of THE SOCIAL CONTRACT was

    A. Hobbes
    B. Locke
    C. Rousseau
    D. Hegel
    E. Marx

21. The author of A TREATISE OF HUMAN NATURE is

    A. Locke
    B. Hobbes
    C. Rousseau
    D. Hume
    E. Berkeley

22. A *hypothetical imperative* claims that

    A. everything we want is only for something else
    B. life is tentative and therefore hypothetical
    C. if you want one thing, you must do another
    D. some things are desired for themselves
    E. none of the above

23. The law of identity
    I. cannot be false
    II. can be true
    III. must be true
    IV. is an a priori truth
    V. all of the above

    The CORRECT answer is:

    A. I, III, IV
    B. I, IV
    C. II, IV
    D. III *only*
    E. V *only*

24. The Enlightenment was characterized by

    A. love, emotion and faith
    B. reason, logic and math
    C. capitalism
    D. feudalism
    E. none of the above

25. The Renaissance was characterized by
    I. philosophical sophistication
    II. artistic brilliance
    III. specialization
    IV. dilettantes
    V. generalizing

    The CORRECT answer is:

    A. I *only*
    B. I, II, III
    C. II, IV
    D. II, III, IV
    E. III, IV, V

26. One of Germany's MOST famous rationalists is

    A. Nietzsche
    B. Schopenhauer
    C. Schilling
    D. Scheler
    E. Kant

27. LIBERTARIANISM relies upon the views of

    A. Marx
    B. Locke
    C. Aristotle
    D. Hobbes
    E. Machiavelli

28. John Locke is noted for emphasizing

    A. inalienable rights
    B. property rights
    C. labor as allowing property appropriation
    D. life, liberty, and the protection of property
    E. all of the above

29. METAPHYSICS is MOST intimately associated with

   A. ethics
   B. epistemology
   C. ontology
   D. aesthetics
   E. logic

30. The author of the MONODOLOGY is

   A. Descartes
   B. Kant
   C. Maimonides
   D. Leibniz
   E. Fichte

31. EMOTIVISM is the theory that says

   A. everyone believes something different about morality
   B. people are too emotional to do philosophy
   C. if something makes you unhappy, it is wrong
   D. if something makes you happy, it is right
   E. saying something is right means that you like it

32. NEUTRAL MONISM was believed by

   A. G. E. Moore
   B. William James
   C. Bertrand Russell
   D. no one
   E. ancient Greeks

33. A NON SEQUITUR is a statement that
   I. follows logically from some premises
   II. does not follow logically from some premises
   III. makes sense given other statements conjoined with it
   IV. does not make sense
   V. makes people laugh frequently

   The CORRECT answer is:

   A. I, III
   B. II, IV, V
   C. III, V
   D. IV only
   E. V only

34. If God is *omniscient,* it means He is

   A. all-powerful
   B. all-knowing
   C. ever-present
   D. eternal
   E. all of the above

35. If God is *omnipresent,* it means He is

   A. all-powerful
   B. all-knowing
   C. ever-present
   D. eternal
   E. all of the above

36. If God is *omnipotent,* it means He is

   A. all-powerful
   B. all-knowing
   C. ever-present
   D. eternal
   E. all of the above

37. The view that claims that emotions are philosophically valid is

A. materialism
B. idealism
C. rationalism
D. existentialism
E. none of the above

38. The statement "I am lying" is paradoxical because it is
    I. true if it is false
    II. false if it is true
    III. false
    IV. reflexive
    V. none of the above
    The CORRECT answer is:

    A. I only
    B. I, II
    C. II only
    D. III, IV
    E. V only

39. Some of the MOST famous American philosophers are
    I. Rousseau
    II. Locke
    III. Peirce
    IV. Dewey
    V. James
    The CORRECT answer is:

    A. I, II
    B. I, III
    C. I, III, IV
    D. II, IV, V
    E. III, IV, V

40. Among the contemporary European philosophies are
    I. existentialism
    II. structuralism
    III. phenomenology
    IV. Marxism
    V. none of the above
    The CORRECT answer is:

    A. I, II, III, IV
    B. I, III, IV
    C. II, III, IV
    D. II, IV
    E. V only

41. PRAGMATISM is a philosophy that claims that
    I. one should only do what is necessary
    II. consequences of actions ought to be considered when evaluating a theory
    III. empiricism is the best criterion of truth
    IV. idealism is to be rejected
    V. all of the above
    The CORRECT answer is:

    A. I only
    B. I, II, III
    C. II, III, IV
    D. III, IV
    E. V only

42. Famous pragmatists are
    I. Marx
    II. Hegel
    III. Dewey
    IV. Peirce
    V. all of the above
    The CORRECT answer is:

    A. I, II   B. I, III
    C. II, III, IV   D. III, IV
    E. V only

43. Probability is an *essential* feature of
    I. a priori reasoning
    II. a posteriori reasoning
    III. science
    IV. mathematics
    V. all of the above
    The CORRECT answer is:

    A. I, II, III   B. I, III
    C. II, III   D. III, IV
    E. V only

44. The *first* philosopher to discuss psychology was

    A. Plato   B. Aristotle
    C. Plotinus   D. Freud
    E. Bacon

45. PHILOSOPHICAL REALISM states that

    A. things in the world exist independently of humans
    B. the things we get to know are eternal
    C. objects are those things seen by human beings
    D. what we know will help us
    E. what we don't know won't hurt us

46. Bertrand Russell, the famous British philosopher, FIRST became famous for his

    A. aristocratic background   B. rich wife
    C. radical ideas   D. mathematical system
    E. none of the above

47. The famous dictum, "All property is theft," was written by the French philosopher

    A. Rousseau   B. Montaigne
    C. Saint-Simon   D. Comte
    E. none of the above

48. Philosophers who were skeptics include
    I. Aristotle
    II. Descartes
    III. Hume
    IV. Reid
    V. none of the above
    The CORRECT answer is:

    A. I, II
    B. II, III
    C. ii, iii, iv
    D. iii, iv
    E. V

49. Semantics concerns the

    A. tower of Babel
    B. structure of language
    C. meaning of terms
    D. vagueness of conversational language
    E. all of the above

50. A statement is a(n)

    A. sentence that can be proven empirically
    B. sentence that expresses a thought
    C. sentence that can be true or false
    D. sentence that cannot be true or false
    E. exclamation

KEY (CORRECT ANSWERS)

1. E	11. B	21. D	31. E	41. C
2. A	12. A	22. C	32. C	42. D
3. B	13. C	23. A	33. B	43. C
4. C	14. D	24. B	34. B	44. B
5. B	15. E	25. C	35. C	45. A
6. E	16. C	26. E	36. A	46. D
7. D	17. E	27. B	37. D	47. C
8. E	18. D	28. E	38. B	48. B
9. A	19. E	29. C	39. E	49. C
10. C	20. C	30. D	40. A	50. C

TEST 2

DIRECTIONS: Each question or incomplete statement is followed by several suggested answers or completions. Select the one that BEST answers the question or completes the statement. *PRINT THE LETTER OF THE CORRECT ANSWER IN THE SPACE AT THE RIGHT.*

1. SOLIPSISM is a view that claims that

    A. everyone else is a figment of my imagination
    B. only I exist
    C. my own existence is the only one I can prove
    D. probably other people exist
    E. all of the above

2. The SOCRATIC METHOD *primarily* consists of

    A. antagonizing others by preaching at them
    B. asking questions
    C. asking atheistic questions
    D. talking to Plato
    E. writing dialogues

3. SOPHISTRY is

    A. the art of language manipulation
    B. the practice of teaching for money
    C. the art of cross-examination
    D. knowing many things
    E. pretending to be ignorant

4. STATE-OF-NATURE theory is another name for

    A. utilitarianism   B. socialism
    C. capitalism   D. utopianism
    E. contract theory

5. A STOIC is a person who believes that

    A. only through suffering can we learn anything
    B. pleasures of the body are evil
    C. happiness comes primarily through knowledge
    D. ignorance is bliss
    E. none of the above

6. SUBJECTIVE IDEALISM claims that
    I.   a person's own standards are what ought to guide him/her
    II. our experience of the real world is what gives us knowledge
    III. the entire world exists primarily through our mind to perceive something is to know it all of the above

    The CORRECT answer is:

    A. I *only*   B. I, II
    C. II, III   D. III, IV
    E. V *only*

10

7. SUBSTANCE is one of the *primary* concepts in

   A. epistemology
   B. aesthetics
   C. political philosophy
   D. metaphysics
   E. theology

8. The "sunnum bonum," a frequently used concept in ethics, means the

   A. happiness of the greatest number
   B. optimal efficiency for the whole society
   C. most pleasure for the individual involved
   D. highest good
   E. all of the above

9. A *teleological* theory is one that emphasizes
   I. motives
   II. actions
   III. consequences
   IV. natural propensities
   V. purposes
   The CORRECT answer is:

   A. I, II
   B. I, II, III
   C. II, III, IV
   D. II, IV, V
   E. IV, V

10. "Bachelors are unmarried men" is an example of a(n)

    A. irrelevant claim
    B. insult to bachelors
    C. tautology
    D. contradiction
    E. none of the above

11. 1. All pigs are green.
    2. Harvey is a pig.
    3. Therefore, Harvey is green.
    The preceding syllogis is

    A. valid
    B. sound
    C. neither valid nor sound
    D. both valid and sound
    E. valid and unsound

12. Something has *intrinsic* value if it has

    A. an emotional connotation for the individual
    B. value in itself
    C. value in the consequences it brings
    D. value according to society
    E. none of the above

13. Something has *extrinsic* value if it has

    A. an emotional connotation for the individual
    B. value in itself
    C. value in the consequences it brings
    D. value according to society
    E. none of the above

14. The philosopher responsible for claiming that this is the "best of all possible worlds" is   14._____

    A. Aristotle   B. Plato
    C. Descartes   D. Leibniz
    E. St. Anselm

15. The philosopher and dramatist who *satirized* the view of the "best of all possible worlds" was   15._____

    A. Voltaire   B. Euripides
    C. Hume   D. Sophocles
    E. Shakespeare

16. A *weltanschauung* is a   16._____

    A. bizarre perspective on life
    B. philosophical position requiring scholarly research
    C. German dessert
    D. worldview
    E. none of the above

17. The philosopher who became well-known for discussing "language games" is   17._____

    A. Bertrand Russell   B. David Hume
    C. G. E. Moore   D. Herbert Spencer
    E. Ludwig Wittgenstein

18. BEING AND NOTHINGNESS was written by   18._____

    A. Camus   B. Heidegger
    C. Sartre   D. Wittgenstein
    E. none of the above

19. An advocate of sociobiology is   19._____

    A. Bertrand Russell   B. Ludwig Wittgenstein
    C. Edmund Wilson   D. Jean-Paul Sartre
    E. Eric Fromm

20. The famous, though short, book THE MEDITATIONS, was written by   20._____

    A. Pascal   B. Descartes
    C. Hume   D. Camus
    E. none of the above

21. An advocate of free will who was OPPOSED to determinism was   21._____

    A. Skinner   B. Freud
    C. Sartre   D. Hume
    E. none of the above

22. An advocate of determinism who was OPPOSED to free will was   22._____

    A. Skinner   B. Freud
    C. Sartre   D. Hume
    E. none of the above

23. The NICHOMACHEAN ETHICS was written by   23._____

A. Plato B. Aristotle
C. Descartes D. Plotinus
E. none of the above

24. BEYOND GOOD AND EVIL was written by

   A. Kierkegaard B. Descartes
   C. Russell D. Nietzsche
   E. Schopenhauer

25. The book ON LIBERTY, very influential in early American legal theory, was written by
      I. Jeremy Bentham
      II. David Hume
      III. John Locke
      IV. John Stuart Mill
      V. John Stuart Mill and Harriet Taylor
    The CORRECT answer is:

   A. I only B. II only
   C. III, IV D. III, IV, V
   E. IV, V

26. A behaviorist famous for his experiments with pigeons was

   A. Watson B. Pavlov
   C. Skinner D. Freud
   E. none of the above

27. A behaviorist famous for his experiments with dogs was

   A. Watson B. Pavlov
   C. Skinner D. Freud
   E. none of the above

28. A fundamental advocate of LOGICAL POSITIVISM was

   A. Ludwig Wittgenstein B. David Hume
   C. John Dewey D. William James
   E. A. J. Ayer

29. The American philosopher *most* associated with EMOTIVISM was

   A. G. E. Moore B. William James
   C. John Dewey D. C. L. Stevenson
   E. none of the above

30. Isaac Newton is well-known for his works on

   A. philosophy B. mathematics
   C. astrology D. physics
   E. all of the above

31. Philosophical reasoning carefully AVOIDS

   A. superstition B. supernatural entities
   C. emotion D. fallacies
   E. all of the above

32. The ancient Greek philosopher who claimed that the primordial element of the universe was water was

    A. Aristotle   B. Epictetus
    C. Socrates   D. Plato
    E. Thales

33. Socrates ended his life by
       I. hanging himself
      II. committing suicide
     III. being condemned by the state
     IV. drinking hemlock
      V. being thrown to lions

The CORRECT answer is:

    A. I, II   B. II, III
    C. III, IV   D. III, V
    E. V *only*

34. Socrates likened himself to a

    A. god   B. humble peasant
    C. noble lord   D. gadfly
    E. none of the above

35. The subjects Socrates was interested in were
       I. friends and pleasure
      II. talking and drinking
     III. truth and beauty
     IV. justice and virtue
      V. all of the above

The CORRECT answer is:

    A. I, II, III   B. III, IV
    C. IV *only*   D. V *only*
    E. none of the above

36. According to Hobbes, no man can be required to

    A. obey the government   B. keep his promises
    C. act self-destructively   D. share his goods with others
    E. all of the above

37. Hobbes claimed that justice can be obtained

    A. only through benevolence
    B. only with loved ones
    C. only in civil society
    D. only in the state of nature
    E. never

38. TWO TREATISES ON CIVIL GOVERNMENT were written by

    A. Rene Descartes   B. John Locke
    C. Thomas Hobbes   D. Jeremy Bentham
    E. Benjamin Franklin

39. According to John Locke, a person acquires personal property by

    A. taking it from others
    B. asking God for use of it
    C. needing it very much
    D. mixing his labor with it
    E. none of the above

40. According to Hobbes, life without a government would be

    A. easygoing and fun
    B. nasty, brutish and short
    C. disorganized and chaotic
    D. creative
    E. all of the above

41. According to Hobbes, humans are by nature
    I.   selfish and greedy
    II. arrogant and nasty
    III. friendly and cooperative
    IV. sociable and passive
    V.   healthy and happy

    The CORRECT answer is:

    A. I, II
    B. II only
    C. III only
    D. III, IV
    E. III, IV, V

42. According to Rousseau, humans are by nature
    I.   selfish and greedy
    II. arrogant and nasty
    III. friendly and cooperative
    IV. sociable and passive
    V.   healthy and happy

    The CORRECT answer is:

    A. I only
    B. I, II
    C. II only
    D. III, IV
    E. III, IV, V

43. According to Freud, humans are by nature
    I.   selfish and greedy
    II. arrogant and nasty
    III. friendly and cooperative
    IV. sociable and passive
    V.   healthy and happy

    The CORRECT answer is:

    A. I only
    B. I, II
    C. III only
    D. III, IV, V
    E. V only

44. The concept of the "general will" is *crucial* to the philosophy of

    A. Hobbes
    B. Hume
    C. Rousseau
    D. Locke
    E. none of the above

45. A famous American thinker who *defended* American Independence from Great Britain was
    I. Thomas Paine
    II. Thomas Jefferson
    III. Benjamin Franklin
    IV. Herbert Spencer
    V. all of the above
    The CORRECT answer is:

    A. I, II, III
    B. I, III, IV
    C. II, III
    D. III, IV
    E. V *only*

46. A famous British thinker who *refuted* Thomas Paine's ideas was

    A. John Stuart Mill
    B. Jeremy Bentham
    C. Richard Price
    D. Edmund Burke
    E. none of the above

47. The American thinker responsible for popularizing the idea of civil disobedience was

    A. Thomas Jefferson
    B. George Washington
    C. Benjamin Franklin
    D. John Adams
    E. Henry David Thoreau

48. The book WALDEN POND was written by

    A. B. F. Skinner
    B. Thomas Jefferson
    C. John Quincy Adams
    D. Henry David Thoreau
    E. none of the above

49. In WALDEN POND, the MAIN subject of discussion was

    A. fish
    B. solitude
    C. thinking and writing
    D. religion
    E. taxation

50. A civil disobedient *purposely* breaks the law in order to

    A. cause trouble
    B. reform an unjust law
    C. change the system
    D. create social unrest
    E. all of the above

KEY (CORRECT ANSWERS)

1. C	11. E	21. C	31. E	41. A
2. B	12. B	22. A	32. E	42. E
3. A	13. C	23. B	33. C	43. B
4. E	14. D	24. D	34. D	44. C
5. C	15. A	25. E	35. B	45. C
6. D	16. D	26. C	36. C	46. D
7. D	17. E	27. B	37. C	47. E
8. D	18. C	28. E	38. B	48. D
9. E	19. C	29. D	39. D	49. E
10. C	20. B	30. E	40. B	50. B

EXAMINATION SECTION
TEST 1

DIRECTIONS: Each question or incomplete statement is followed by several suggested answers or completions. Select the one that BEST answers the question or completes the statement. *PRINT THE LETTER OF THE CORRECT ANSWER IN THE SPACE AT THE RIGHT.*

1. Utilitarianism is a very democratic moral theory because
    I. it does not rely upon judgments by experts
    II. it stipulates that everyone's utility be counted
    III. it stipulates that everyone determine his/her own utility
    IV. it rules out foolish or imprudent wishes and desires
    V. it rules out considerations of intentions
   The CORRECT answer is:

   A. I, II, IV
   B. I, II
   C. I, II, III
   D. II, III
   E. II, III, IV

   1.____

2. The STRONG points of utilitarianism include
    I. its reliance on objective data
    II. its reliance on subjective data
    III. the fact that it applies to any and all situations
    IV. the fact that it prescribes a certain, 4-step procedure to determine what ought to be done, morally speaking
    V. its encouragement of social reforms
   The CORRECT answer is:

   A. I, III
   B. III, V
   C. I, III, V
   D. I, IV, V
   E. I, III, IV, V

   2.____

3. The WEAK points of utilitarianism include
    I. its 4-step decision procedure
    II. its reliance on subjective data
    III. its reliance on objective data
    IV. that it applies to any and all situations
    V. its encouragement of social reforms
   The CORRECT answer is:

   A. I, III, IV
   B. I, II, IV
   C. I, II, V
   D. I, IV, V
   E. I, II, III

   3.____

4. The utilitarianism decision procedure requires that each person
    I. figure out the consequences of each alternative action
    II. figure out which actions are available at the time
    III. figure out how much happiness each alternative will bring about
    IV. figure out how to maximize the happiness of everyone
    V. deliberate rationally over each act he/she performs
   The CORRECT answer is:

   4.____

19

A. I, III B. I, II, III
C. I, III, V D. I, II, III, V
E. all of the above

5. According to Kant,
   I. lying is always wrong
   II. lying is usually wrong, except in certain extreme situations
   III. lying is the kind of action that harms people
   IV. lying can lead to better consequences than not lying in some cases
   V. lying cannot lead to better consequences than not lying in any case
   The CORRECT answer is:

   A. I, III B. II, III
   C. I, II D. I, II, III
   E. I, III, IV

6. According to John Stuart Mill,
   I. lying is always wrong
   II. lying is usually wrong, except in certain extremesituations
   III. lying is the kind of action that harms people
   IV. lying can lead to better consequences than not lying in some cases
   V. lying cannot lead to better consequences than not lying in any case
   The CORRECT answer is:

   A. I, II B. II, III
   C. II, IV D. I, II, IV
   E. II, III, IV

7. Utilitarianism is opposed to paternalism because
   I. it allows others to decide how happy a certain actionwill make an individual
   II. it does not allow others to decide how happy a certain action will make an individual
   III. it goes by majority rule
   IV. it presupposes that utility is subjective
   V. it presupposes that utility is objective
   The CORRECT answer is:

   A. I, II B. II, III
   C. II, IV D. I, III, IV
   E. II, III, IV

8. Deontology is opposed to paternalism because
   I. it insists that individuals retain rights
   II. it insists that each person should act according to his/her conscience
   III. it insists that everyone ought to help others, even when others do not wish it
   IV. autonomy requires free will in decision-making
   V. all of the above
   The CORRECT answer is:

   A. I, II, III B. I, II, V
   C. I, II D. I, II, IV
   E. II, IV

9. Paternalism states that

   A. everyone *always* ought to decide what is best for himself/herself as well as for others
   B. it is sometimes right *not* to decide what is best for oneself and others
   C. it is *never* right to decide what is best for oneself and others
   D. it is *justifiable* to go against others' wishes if it is for their own good
   E. it is *not* justifiable to go against others' wishes even if it is for their own good

10. Ethical absolutism is a type of theory that claims:
    I. If an action is wrong at any one time, it is always wrong
    II. Values vary in different cultures
    III. It is morally wrong to make exceptions to moral rules
    IV. It is morally justified to make exceptions to moral rules only if doing so is commanded by a legitimate authority
    V. Relativism is incoherent and/or immoral

    The CORRECT answer is:

    A. I, III   B. III, V
    C. I, V   D. I, III, V
    E. I, III, IV, V

11. An absolutist ethical theory was held by

    A. Jeremy Bentham   B. John Stuart Mill
    C. Immanuel Kant   D. Charles Stevenson
    E. all of the above

12. The Harm Principle states that

    A. only determining the consequences of an act reveals whether that act is harmful or not
    B. actions that harm are prima facie wrong
    C. actions that harm are wrong
    D. morality presupposes that everyone wants to avoid harming others
    E. the only criterion of moral rightness is avoiding harm

13. Skepticism is a theory that states that

    A. people frequently have ulterior motives for doing good actions
    B. things usually turn out for the worst
    C. knowledge is impossible
    D. philosphical conclusions are only a matter of opinion
    E. all of the above

14. Skeptical views were developed by
    I. Plato
    II. Aristotle
    III. Descartes
    IV. Hume
    V. Kant

    The CORRECT answer is:

    A. III, IV   B. I, III
    C. I, IV   D. III, IV, V
    E. II, III, IV

15. Hume became famous for advocating that
    I. miracles are not impossible
    II. miracles are impossible
    III. the principle of cause and effect is unfounded
    IV. the principle of cause and effect is important and useful
    V. that the existence of miracles does not justify faith in God
    The CORRECT answer is:

    A. I, III, V
    B. II, III, IV
    C. I, II, III
    D. II, III, V
    E. none of the above

16. Hume's epistemological theory may be *correctly* called
    I. empiricist
    II. idealist
    III. materialist
    IV. determinist
    V. rationalist
    The CORRECT answer is:

    A. I, II, III
    B. I, III, V
    C. I, III
    D. II, IV
    E. I, III, IV

17. Kant's epistemological theory may be *correctly* called
    I. empiricist
    II. idealist
    III. materialist
    IV. determinist
    V. rationalist
    The CORRECT answer is:

    A. I, III
    B. I, V
    C. I, II, III
    D. II, III, V
    E. II, V

18. Descartes' epistemological theory may be *correctly* called
    I. empiricist
    II. idealist
    III. materialist
    IV. determinist
    V. rationalist
    The CORRECT answer is:

    A. I, II, III
    B. I, III, V
    C. I, II, V
    D. II, IV
    E. II, V

19. Rights are an important concept in one of the following moral theories:

    A. Utilitarianism
    B. Deontology
    C. Emotivism
    D. Relativism
    E. Egoism

20. Egoism is a moral theory that states that

    A. everyone always acts so as to maximize his/her own self-interest
    B. everyone always ought to act so as to maximize his/her own self-interest
    C. doing what is good for others requires self-sacrifice
    D. altruistic acts are few and far between
    E. All of the above

21. Egoistic ethical theory includes the following claims:
    I. Self-interest is the only worthwhile motive for doing an act
    II. Altruistic acts are always done to promote self-interest
    III. Human beings are rational in that they seek to maximize their own self-interest
    IV. God helps those who help themselves
    V. To be morally good, all we need to do is be prudent

    The CORRECT answer is:

    A. I, II, III   B. I, II, III, IV
    C. I, II, III, V   D. II, III, V
    E. All of the above

22. Egoism as a moral theory was advocated by

    A. Aristotle   B. Plato
    C. Kant   D. Hobbes
    E. Hume

23. Psychological egoism states that
    I. everyone always ought to promote his/her own self-interest
    II. no one should try to promote another person's self-interest
    III. everyone always tries to promote his/her own self-interest
    IV. everyone usually tries to promote his/her own self-interest
    V. no one ever tries to promote another person's self-interest

    The CORRECT answer is:

    A. II, III   B. III, V
    C. III, IV, V   D. II, III, V
    E. I, III, V

24. Some fields that assume psychological egoism are
    I. psychology
    II. political science
    III. economics
    IV. literature
    V. religion

    The CORRECT answer is:

    A. I, II   B. II, III
    C. II, III, IV   D. II, III, V
    E. II, IV

25. Philosophers who have emphasized the importance of habit in human behavior is(are)
    I. Plato
    II. Aristotle
    III. Hume
    IV. Hobbes
    V. Descartes
    The CORRECT answer is:

    A. I only
    B. II only
    C. I, II
    D. I, III
    E. II, III

26. Epicurus is famed for his theory concerning
    I. good food
    II. Epicurean delights other than good food
    III. hedonism
    IV. living a life that brings peace of mind
    V. all of the above
    The CORRECT answer is:

    A. I, III
    B. I, IV
    C. III, IV
    D. II, III
    E. II, III, IV

27. Epicurus' version of moral theory recommends
    I. not getting angry at frustrating situations
    II. avoiding scholarly work because it leads to unhappiness
    III. studying science as much as possible to understand reality
    IV. living on bread and water to become healthy
    V. eating good food for pleasure and happiness
    The CORRECT answer is:

    A. I, II
    B. I, II, V
    C. III, IV
    D. I, II, III
    E. I, II, IV

28. An "analytical" statement is *one* that

    A. requires deep philosophical reflection
    B. requires the use of mathematics
    C. provides information about the world
    D. defines a term
    E. cannot be false

29. A "synthetic" statement is *one* that

    A. is invented by a person
    B. requires the use of mathematics
    C. provides information about the world
    D. defines a term
    E. cannot be false

30. A "synthetic a priori" statement is one that is   30.____

    A. informative and provides a definition
    B. *not* informative and provides a definition
    C. informative and provides no definition
    D. informative and cannot be false
    E. informative and may or may not be false

31. According to David Hume, our notion that similar causes bring about similar effects is   31.____
    really reducible to
        I.   wishful thinking
        II. practical experience
        III. custom and habit
        IV. ancient philosophical ideas
        V.   all of the above
    The CORRECT answer is:

    A. II, III   B. I, III
    C. III, IV   D. I, II, III
    E. I, II, III, IV

32. The allegory of the cave, in Plato's REPUBLIC, concerns   32.____
        I.   slaves rebelling against their masters
        II. epistemological problems of knowledge and illusion
        III. psychological habits and beliefs
        IV. the danger of thinking philosophically
        V.   people's natural impulse to learn as much as possible
    The CORRECT answer is:

    A. I, II, III   B. II, III, V
    C. I, III, V   D. II, III
    E. II, III, IV

33. In his book ON LIBERTY, John Stuart Mill argued that   33.____
        I.   the majority should make moral and political decisions, Nnot an elite group
        II. individuals have rights against other individuals and minorities
        III. individuals ought to go along with the majority
        IV. in democratic societies, governments ought not to meddle with individuals
             who are not harming others
        V.   individuals are subject to the tyranny of the majority
    The CORRECT answer is:

    A. IV, V   B. I, II
    C. I, IV   D. III, IV
    E. III, IV, V

34. John Stuart Mill attributes most of the ideas in ON LIBERTY to   34.____

    A. Jeremy Bentham   B. James Mill (his father)
    C. Harriet Taylor   D. David Hume
    E. John Locke

35. Plato thought that virtue was
    I. the most important thing in life
    II. difficult to define
    III. something you should teach to children from an early age
    IV. something that cannot be taught
    V. achieved if and when justice was achieved
    The CORRECT answer is:

    A. II, IV   B. I, II
    C. I, II, III   D. I, II, IV
    E. I, IV

36. The "use/mention" distinction is important because
    I. it permits the analysis of meaning
    II. we sometimes talk about a word
    III. it requires using inverted commas
    IV. it helps philosophical analysis
    V. otherwise we will commit equivocations
    The CORRECT answer is:

    A. I, II   B. II, IV
    C. I, III, V   D. I, II, IV, V
    E. all of the above

37. "Meta-ethics" concerns
    A. moral judgments about what is right and what is wrong
    B. empirical judgments about moral beliefs
    C. philosophical analysis of moral terms
    D. logical critiques of philosophical arguments in ethics
    E. all of the above

38. Stipulative definitions are definitions that
    I. specify the meaning of a term according to the author
    II. use standard specifications of meaning such as a dictionary
    III. rely upon standard usage of a language
    IV. create uniformity and standard usage
    V. are designed to clarify complex problems
    The CORRECT answer is:

    A. I, II   B. IV, V
    C. I, III, V   D. I, IV, V
    E. I, V

39. Theology involves
    I. epistemological distinctions
    II. metaphysical claims
    III. study of religious dogma
    IV. philosophy of religion
    V. theoretical justifications of religious beliefs
    The CORRECT answer is:

    A. I, II, III   B. II, III, IV
    C. I, III, V   D. I, III, IV
    E. III, IV, V

40. A criticism of utilitarianism as a moral theory is

   A. that it requires a knowledge of the future to make a decision
   B. that it makes the same action right at one time and wrong at another
   C. that it is unjust
   D. that it is very time-consuming
   E. all of the above

41. The problem with the following statement, "It is wrong to make moral judgments" is that

   A. we do so all the time
   B. it is arrogant
   C. it is a contradiction
   D. it leads to apathy
   E. All of the above

42. According to Aristotle, an enthymeme is

   A. a form of rhetorical argument
   B. a common method of persuasion
   C. ruled out in legal arguments
   D. a syllogism missing a premise
   E. All of the above

43. Playing "Devil's Advocate" requires that a person

   A. study religious dogma to know what the Devil believes
   B. retain a firm hold on his/her beliefs
   C. argue against his/her own opinion for the sake of the argument
   D. follow Socrates' example and ask questions all the time
   E. All of the above

44. The art of forensics involves
   I. chemical analysis of criminal evidence
   II. arguments for and against someone accused of something
   III. debating
   IV. logical prowess
   V. All of the above
   The CORRECT answer is:

   A. II, III, IV
   B. I, II, III
   C. III, IV, V
   D. II, III
   E. III, IV

45. Included in Aristotle's list of the ingredients for happiness is(are):
   I. High social station
   II. Friends, children
   III. Athletic ability
   IV. Beautiful looks
   V. Money
   The CORRECT answer is:

   A. I only
   B. II only
   C. III only
   D. IV only
   E. all of the above

46. An oligarchy is a form of government in which

   A. only the elite rule
   B. only aristocrats rule
   C. kings and nobility rule
   D. property owners rule
   E. no one rules

47. According to Marx and Engels,
   I.   capitalism was a liberating influence in its early days
   II. society is the history of class struggles
   III. dominant classes inevitably win out in political struggles
   IV. labor is intrinsically immoral under capitalism
   V.   all of the above
   The CORRECT answer is:

   A. I, III, V
   B. I, II
   C. II, IV
   D. I, II, IV
   E. I, II, III

48. John Locke provided a justification of
   I.   the modern state
   II. private property
   III. separating God from the government
   IV. owning apples one has picked oneself
   V.   all of the above
   The CORRECT answer is:

   A. I, II
   B. II, III
   C. II, IV, V
   D. I, II, IV
   E. II, IV

49. Among the "natural rights" emphasized by John Locke is (are):
   I.   The right to keep what one has labored for
   II. The right to pursue happiness
   III. The right to have one's property protected by government
   IV. The right to control our own persons
   V.   All of the above
   The CORRECT answer is:

   A. I, II, III
   B. II, III, IV
   C. I, III, IV
   D. I, II, III, IV
   E. V only

50. *One* of the MAIN concepts in existentialism, as promoted by Jean-Paul Sartre, is

   A. pessimism
   B. futility
   C. suicide
   D. choice
   E. faith

KEY (CORRECT ANSWERS)

1.	C	11.	C	21.	C	31.	A	41.	E
2.	E	12.	B	22.	D	32.	E	42.	D
3.	B	13.	C	23.	B	33.	A	43.	C
4.	E	14.	A	24.	B	34.	C	44.	A
5.	A	15.	D	25.	E	35.	D	45.	E
6.	C	16.	E	26.	C	36.	D	46.	D
7.	C	17.	E	27.	C	37.	C	47.	D
8.	D	18.	E	28.	D	38.	E	48.	D
9.	D	19.	B	29.	C	39.	E	49.	C
10.	D	20.	B	30.	D	40.	E	50.	D

TEST 2

DIRECTIONS: Each question or incomplete statement is followed by several suggested answers or completions. Select the one that BEST answers the question or completes the statement. *PRINT THE LETTER OF THE CORRECT ANSWER IN THE SPACE AT THE RIGHT.*

1. The view that each thing or person tends toward a goal or purpose is
    I. emotivism
    II. functionalism
    III. teleology
    IV. idealism
    V. materialism
   The CORRECT answer is:

   A. I only
   B. II only
   C. III, IV
   D. II, III
   E. IV, V

   1.____

2. The philosopher FIRST responsible for a teleological view of life is
    I. Plato
    II. Socrates
    III. Aristotle
    IV. Heraclitus
    V. Democritus
   The CORRECT answer is:

   A. I only
   B. I, II
   C. III only
   D. IV only
   E. V only

   2.____

3. The philosopher frequently called a "peripatetic" and whose Academy was also referred to as "The Peripatetic" school was
    I. Plato
    II. Socrates
    III. Aristotle
    IV. Heraclitus
    V. Plotinus
   The CORRECT answer is:

   A. I only
   B. II only
   C. I, II
   D. III only
   E. IV, V

   3.____

4. The view that society is composed of an aggregate of units is called
    I. functionalism
    II. teleology
    III. collectivism
    IV. organicism
    V. individualism
   The CORRECT answer is:

   A. I only
   B. I, II
   C. III only
   D. IV only
   E. V only

   4.____

30

5. The view that society is comprised of integrally related parts and that the whole is greater than the sum of its parts is called
   I. functionalism
   II. teleology
   III. collectivism
   IV. organicism
   V. individualism
   The CORRECT answer is:

   A. I, II
   B. III only
   C. III, IV
   D. IV only
   E. V only

6. Philosophers who were organicists were
   I. Democritus
   II. Aristotle
   III. Bentham
   IV. Hegel
   V. Marx
   The CORRECT answer is:

   A. I only
   B. I, II
   C. III only
   D. II, IV, V
   E. IV only

7. Philosophers who were individualists were
   I. Heraclitus
   II. Aristotle
   III. Bentham
   IV. Hegel
   V. Marx
   The CORRECT answer is:

   A. I only
   B. I, II
   C. III only
   D. IV, V
   E. V only

8. Philosophers who agreed that happiness was the *primary* goal in human life are
   I. Socrates
   II. Aristotle
   III. Descartes
   IV. Bentham
   V. John Stuart Mill
   The CORRECT answer is:

   A. I only
   B. I, III
   C. II only
   D. II, IV, V
   E. IV, V

9. Plato and Aristotle *primarily* DISAGREED about the philosophical issue of
   I. empirical evidence
   II. cosmology
   III. politics
   IV. whether virtue was attainable
   V. aesthetics
   The CORRECT answer is:

   A. I *only*
   B. II *only*
   C. I, II, V
   D. II, IV
   E. III *only*

10. Aristotle emphasized, in direct contrast to Plato, that
    I. most people should train in philosophy
    II. people ought to actively pursue goals
    III. studying virtue is the best thing to do
    IV. individual acts have great moral significance
    V. universal goodness is the source of each good action
    The CORRECT answer is:

    A. I *only*
    B. II, III
    C. IV *only*
    D. II, III, IV
    E. II, V

11. The philosopher in ancient Greece who thought that a person who is ugly, poor, and without children has little chance of being happy is
    I. Socrates
    II. Plato
    III. Aristotle
    IV. Pythagoras
    V. Plotinus
    The CORRECT answer is:

    A. I *only*
    B. I, II
    C. III *only*
    D. III, IV
    E. IV, V

12. Philosophers who thought that studying morality is worthwhile only if it makes the student more ethical are
    I. Plato
    II. Aristotle
    III. Hegel
    IV. Descartes
    V. Marx
    The CORRECT answer is:

    A. I *only*
    B. I, III
    C. II, IV
    D. II, V
    E. III, V

13. The philosopher MOST responsible for the idea that the good life is that which emphasizes moderation, i.e., "the mean between the extremes," is
    I. Plato
    II. Aristotle
    III. Hegel
    IV. Leibniz
    V. Spinoza
    The CORRECT answer is:

    A. I only
    B. II only
    C. I, III
    D. III, IV
    E. V only

14. "Pyrrhonism" refers to a philosophy emphasizing
    I. love
    II. justice
    III. asceticism
    IV. heroic skepticism
    V. hedonism
    The CORRECT answer is:

    A. I only
    B. I, II
    C. III only
    D. III, IV
    E. IV, V

15. Pythagoreans emphasized in their philosophy that
    I. happiness is the goal of life
    II. the pure life was the best
    III. philosophical discussion is preferable to silence
    IV. silence is preferable to philosophical discussion
    V. asceticism is desirable
    The CORRECT answer is:

    A. I only
    B. I, V
    C. II only
    D. III, V
    E. II, IV, V

16. Axiology is that realm of philosophy which concerns
    I. metaphysics
    II. reality
    III. love and justice
    IV. goodness
    V. pleasure
    The CORRECT answer is:

    A. I only
    B. I, II
    C. III only
    D. IV only
    E. V only

17. *Basic* features of philosophy include
    I. generality
    II. logic
    III. emotion
    IV. particularity
    V. interpretation
    The CORRECT answer is:

    A. I, III
    B. II *only*
    C. I, II, IV
    D. I, II, V
    E. III, IV

18. A noteworthy medieval philosopher was

    A. Plato
    B. Hobbes
    C. Augustine
    D. Plotinus
    E. Thucydides

19. Modern philosophers, as compared to ancient and medieval philosophers, emphasize
    I. theology
    II. metaphysical speculation
    III. logical analysis
    IV. linguistic analysis
    V. ordinary language
    The CORRECT answer is:

    A. I *only*
    B. I, II
    C. III *only*
    D. III, IV
    E. III, IV, V

20. Studying philosophy contributes to one's life in that it
    I. fosters intellectual growth
    II. reaffirms one's early beliefs
    III. is culturally enriching
    IV. guarantees that one will be wary of falsehoods
    V. satisfies our curiosity
    The CORRECT answer is:

    A. I, III, V
    B. II, IV
    C. I, III, IV
    D. II, III, IV
    E. II, V

21. Some characteristics of the deductive method in philosophy are that it
    I. is intuitive
    II. generates highly probable conclusions
    III. generates certain conclusions
    IV. uses axioms
    V. relies upon empirical data
    The CORRECT answer is:

    A. I, III, IV
    B. II, V
    C. III, IV
    D. III, V
    E. II, III, IV, V

22. The primary difference between ontology and cosmology is that
    I. the former is logically independent of the latter
    II. one is concerned with being and the other with conclusions
    III. the latter is concerned with origins and the former with what is
    IV. only one is fundamentally connected to metaphysics
    V. only one concerns the origins of the universe
    The CORRECT answer is:

    A. I only   B. II, IV
    C. I, III, V   D. III, V
    E. IV, V

23. One MAJOR difference between materialism and idealism is that
    I. only one represents a major philosophical school
    II. the latter includes a non-physical element
    III. the former includes no supersensible rationale
    IV. the ancients only studied the latter
    V. only one is in accordance with common sense
    The CORRECT answer is:

    A. I, II   B. II only
    C. I, IV   D. II, III
    E. III, IV, V

24. The FIRST philosopher to claim that planets moved in an elliptical, not circular, manner was
    I. Democritus
    II. Ptolemy
    III. Galileo
    IV. Copernicus
    V. Descartes
    The CORRECT answer is:

    A. I only   B. II only
    C. III, IV   D. III only
    E. IV, V

25. The view that all of reality can be reduced to one substance or entity is
    I. monism
    II. dualism
    III. idealism
    IV. animism
    V. pantheism
    The CORRECT answer is:

    A. I only   B. I, III
    C. II only   D. III only
    E. IV, V

26. Philosophers who are "pluralists" are those who claim that
    I. no one knows what is true or false
    II. seeing is believing
    III. material reality is reducible to more than one element
    IV. material reality is reducible to one element
    V. there is no such thing as material reality
    The CORRECT answer is:

    A. I only
    B. I, III
    C. III only
    D. IV only
    E. V only

27. Frequently, monists *also* claim that
    I. only minds or spirits are real
    II. philosophy should be abandoned for science
    III. material reality is an illusion
    IV. appearance is more important than reality
    V. reality is more important than appearance
    The CORRECT answer is:

    A. I only
    B. I, II
    C. III only
    D. I, III, IV
    E. none of the above

28. One claim *frequently* put forth by "animists" is that
    I. only animals embody religious spirits
    II. living plants and animals each represent God directly
    III. living plants and animals have a special spirit
    IV. living plants and animals are at man's disposal
    V. humans are the only creatures animated by God's spirit
    The CORRECT answer is:

    A. I only
    B. I, IV
    C. II, III
    D. III, V
    E. IV only

29. The fundamental meaning of "hylozoism" is represented by the view that
    I. water is the creative force of the universe
    II. life is inseparable from matter
    III. life must be separated from inanimate matter
    IV. atomic particulars are the nucleus of matter
    V. there is no such thing as inanimate matter
    The CORRECT answer is:

    A. I only
    B. I, II
    C. II, V
    D. III, IV
    E. IV, V

30. The Latin phrase "sui generis" *usually* refers to
    I. self-generation
    II. soft cells in atomic matter
    III. the generation of animal life
    IV. God's existence
    V. human existence
    The CORRECT answer is:

    A. I *only*
    B. II *only*
    C. I, III
    D. I, IV
    E. I, III, V

31. The cosmological theory called "archebiosis" refers to the view that
    I. most natural conditions are created by God's will
    II. nature is largely the result of a chance combination of events
    III. nature has a rational explanation
    IV. natural life is explainable by teleological purposes
    V. life's origins must remain mysterious to humans
    The CORRECT answer is:

    A. I *only*
    B. II *only*
    C. I, IV
    D. III *only*
    E. V *only*

32. Darwin's fundamental principle of scientific explanation for biological life is
    I. the principle of natural selection
    II. the principle of immutable force
    III. designed to explain extinct species
    IV. rarely verified through empirical evidence
    V. equally applicable to human and legal society
    The CORRECT answer is:

    A. I *only*
    B. II, III
    C. I, III
    D. II, III, IV
    E. IV, V

33. The theological view that challenges Darwin's theory is
    I. primordialism
    II. fundamentalism
    III. episcopalianism
    IV. asceticism
    V. creationism
    The CORRECT answer is:

    A. I *only*
    B. I, III
    C. II *only*
    D. IV, V
    E. II, V

34. According to David Hume, the human mind is

    A. the organizing principle of human life
    B. a collection of perceptions
    C. indubitably given a priori
    D. ultimately indistinguishable from matter
    E. an immaterial substance

35. According to Aristotle, the human mind is
    A. the organizing principle of human life
    B. a collection of perceptions
    C. indubitably given a priori
    D. ultimately indistinguishable from matter
    E. an immaterial substance

36. According to Descartes and Berkeley, the human mind is
    I. the organizing principle of human life
    II. a collection of perceptions
    III. indubitably given a priori
    IV. ultimately indistinguishable from matter
    V. an immaterial substance
    The CORRECT answer is:

    A. I only
    B. I, II
    C. III, V
    D. IV only
    E. I, III, IV

37. If dualism is TRUE, then
    I. none of us know if we have a body
    II. none of us know if we have a mind
    III. the relationship of mind to body remains a question
    IV. Descartes was correct
    V. Marx was correct
    The CORRECT answer is:

    A. I only
    B. I, II
    C. III only
    D. III, IV
    E. V only

38. The theory called "interactionism" claims that
    I. Hegel's theory of history is correct
    II. the mind is separate from the body
    III. the mind and the body are subtly inter-related
    IV. the mind and the body are identical
    V. the mind actually is no more than the brain
    The CORRECT answer is:

    A. I only
    B. II only
    C. III only
    D. I, III
    E. IV, V

39. The theory of mind called "parallelism" claims that
    I. God's will is parallel to man's
    II. minds and bodies never interact
    III. no one knows for sure if the self is intact
    IV. theories of theology amount to the same thing
    V. minds are no more than brains
    The CORRECT answer is:

    A. I only
    B. II only
    C. I, III
    D. IV only
    E. V only

40. The theory of mind called "identity theory" claims that
    I. God's will is identical to man's
    II. no one knows whether the mind is real or not
    III. theories of theology amount to the same thing
    IV. minds and bodies never interact
    V. minds are no more than brains
    The CORRECT answer is:

    A. I only
    B. II only
    C. III only
    D. III, IV
    E. V only

41. The peculiarity of the theory called "epiphenomenalism" in the philosophy of mind is its claim that
    I. the mind is no more than the brain
    II. the body has no independent reality from the mind
    III. the mind has no independent reality from the body
    IV. there are no bodies, only minds
    V. theology is the source of identity
    The CORRECT answer is:

    A. I only
    B. II only
    C. III only
    D. II, IV
    E. V only

42. The theory called "fatalism" claims that
    I. the Fates are in contact with human souls
    II. whatever happens is meant to happen
    III. actions determine to a large extent a person's life
    IV. events are largely uncontrolled by human action
    V. people deserve what they get
    The CORRECT answer is:

    A. I only
    B. I, V
    C. II only
    D. II, IV
    E. III, IV, V

43. The theory called "predestination" claims that
    I. the Fates are in contact with human souls
    II. events that occur are planned by an extra-human force
    III. actions are largely determined by human actions
    IV. what you do has no effect on what happens
    V. there is a force larger than human powers in control of things
    The CORRECT answer is:

    A. I, II
    B. II, III
    C. II, V
    D. II, IV, V
    E. IV, V

44. *Determinism* is the philosophical view that
    I. no one believes could possibly be true
    II. determined people can accomplish anything
    III. human actions are explainable by preceding causes
    IV. human actions are not explainable by preceding causes
    V. serious motivation solves most human problems
    The CORRECT answer is:

    A. I *only*
    B. I, V
    C. II *only*
    D. III, V
    E. III *only*

45. The theory called "indeterminism" claims that
    I. determined people are ineffectual against the fates
    II. human actions are explainable by preceding causes
    III. human actions are not explainable by preceding causes
    IV. humans have free will
    V. God controls human events to a large degree
    The CORRECT answer is:

    A. I *only*
    B. I, III
    C. III, IV
    D. II, V
    E. V *only*

46. The school(s) of thought famous for espousing indeterminism is(are)
    I. existentialism
    II. empiricism
    III. natural law theory
    IV. teleological theory
    V. identity theory
    The CORRECT answer is:

    A. I *only*
    B. I, II
    C. I, III
    D. IV *only*
    E. IV, V

47. The difference between *objective* and *subjective* idealists is that the
    I. former believe in reality, whereas the latter do not
    II. former believe that ideas are eternal
    III. latter believe that reality is independent of the mind
    IV. latter believe that reality is whatever is perceived by minds
    V. former believe that reality is whatever is perceived by minds
    The CORRECT answer is:

    A. I *only*
    B. II, IV
    C. I, III
    D. V *only*
    E. II, III, IV

48. One problem with philosophies based on common sense is that
    I. sticks do not bend when placed in a glass of water
    II. science defies many principles of common sense
    III. so few people have common sense
    IV. philosophical theories are supposed to be complex
    V. they are so plentiful
    The CORRECT answer is:

    A. I only
    B. I, III
    C. I, II
    D. III, IV
    E. IV, V

49. The philosophical school of pragmatism asserts that
    I. learning takes place within a physical environment
    II. people have innate knowledge
    III. appearances are never the same as realities
    IV. experience is fundamental
    V. logic is paramount in learning
    The CORRECT answer is:

    A. I only
    B. I, III
    C. II, III
    D. I, IV
    E. V only

50. John Dewey's form of pragmatism claimed that
    I. knowledge reflects the world
    II. human knowledge reshapes the world
    III. knowledge is an instrumental thing
    IV. knowledge is intrinsically good
    V. science ought to be rejected in favor of pragmatism
    The CORRECT answer is:

    A. I only
    B. II only
    C. I, IV
    D. II, III
    E. V only

KEY (CORRECT ANSWERS)

1. D	11. C	21. C	31. B	41. C
2. C	12. D	22. D	32. C	42. D
3. D	13. B	23. D	33. E	43. D
4. E	14. D	24. B	34. B	44. E
5. C	15. E	25. A	35. A	45. C
6. D	16. D	26. C	36. C	46. C
7. C	17. D	27. E	37. D	47. B
8. D	18. C	28. C	38. C	48. C
9. A	19. E	29. C	39. B	49. D
10. D	20. A	30. D	40. E	50. D

EXAMINATION SECTION
TEST 1

DIRECTIONS: Each question or incomplete statement is followed by several suggested answers or completions. Select the one that BEST answers the question or completes the statement. *PRINT THE LETTER OF THE CORRECT ANSWER IN THE SPACE AT THE RIGHT.*

1. American philosophers include
    I. Bertrand Russell
    II. John Stuart Mill
    III. William James
    IV. John Dewey
    V. Alfred North Whitehead
   The CORRECT answer is:

   A. I *only*
   B. I, II, V
   C. II, IV, V
   D. III, IV, V
   E. II, IV

   1.____

2. Correspondence theory is *primarily* used as a
    I. mathematical assumption
    II. axiomatic presupposition
    III. test of the truth of statements
    IV. limitation on human knowledge
    V. theory of art
   The CORRECT answer is:

   A. I *only*
   B. I, II
   C. III *only*
   D. II, IV
   E. III, V

   2.____

3. Phenomenalism is a theory that claims that
    I. reality is autonomous and independent of human minds
    II. reality is the joint product of minds and sensory data
    III. some philosophers will know what noumena are
    IV. no one ever knows what noumena are
    V. phenomena and noumena are distinguishable
   The CORRECT answer is:

   A. I *only*
   B. II *only*
   C. I, III
   D. II, V
   E. II, IV

   3.____

4. The philosopher *primarily* responsible for distinguishing noumena and phenomena is

   A. Hume
   B. Aristotle
   C. Kant
   D. Descartes
   E. Dewey

   4.____

43

5. The philosophical theory called "coherence theory" is one that
   I. only materialists believe
   II. only idealists believe
   III. relies for its basis on other theories
   IV. emphasizes soundness over validity
   V. emphasizes validity over soundness

   The CORRECT answer is:

   A. II, III
   B. I, IV
   C. I, IV, V
   D. II, III, V
   E. III, V

6. Absolutist theory is *primarily* found in theories concerning

   A. epistemology
   B. metaphysics
   C. ethics
   D. aesthetics
   E. epiphenomenalism

7. The "Theory of the Mean" was created by
   I. Plato
   II. Aristotle
   III. Descartes
   IV. Kant
   V. Mill

   The CORRECT answer is:

   A. I only
   B. II only
   C. II, III
   D. IV only
   E. V only

8. The term "mean" in the moral "Theory of the Mean" refers to a(n)
   I. quantitative relationship
   II. qualitative relationship
   III. absolute figure
   IV. relative figure
   V. low or vulgar person or thing

   The CORRECT answer is:

   A. I only
   B. I, III
   C. I, IV
   D. II, V
   E. V only

9. The term "theologism" refers *primarily* to _____ religious theory.
   I. Hindu
   II. Buddhist
   III. Christian
   IV. Taoist
   V. Confucianist

   The CORRECT answer is:

   A. I only
   B. I, III
   C. II only
   D. III only
   E. I, IV, V

10. The term "formalism" applies BEST to the theory of
    I. Aristotle
    II. Hume
    III. Kant
    IV. Mill
    V. Dewey
    The CORRECT answer is:

    A. I only
    B. II, IV
    C. III only
    D. IV, V
    E. V only

11. Motives are MOST important in the moral theory developed by
    I. Aristotle
    II. Plato
    III. Descartes
    IV. Kant
    V. Mill
    The CORRECT answer is:

    A. I only
    B. II, IV
    C. IV only
    D. III, V
    E. IV, V

12. The term "eudaemonism" in moral theory refers to
    I. pain
    II. pleasure
    III. happiness
    IV. good will
    V. hedonism
    The CORRECT answer is:

    A. I only
    B. I, V
    C. II, III
    D. III only
    E. IV only

13. The cognitivist in moral theory claims that
    I. no one knows what is right and wrong
    II. moral judgments are subjective
    III. moral judgments are largely unprovable
    IV. moral judgments are *either* true or false
    V. moral judgments are *neither* true or false
    The CORRECT answer is:

    A. I only
    B. I, II
    C. III, V
    D. IV only
    E. V only

14. The *primary* concept(s) in the philosophy of aesthetics is(are)
    I. virtue
    II. beauty
    III. goodness
    IV. right
    V. justice

    The CORRECT answer is:

    A. I *only*   B. I, II
    C. III, IV   D. II *only*
    E. IV, V

15. For Plato, the MAJOR problem with art was that it
    I. moved people to drastic action
    II. inspired moral righteousness
    III. was too difficult for all but a few to master
    IV. is too trivial for political philosophy
    V. wasted philosophers' time

    The CORRECT answer is:

    A. V *only*   B. I *only*
    C. II, III   D. III, IV
    E. I, III, V

16. The philosopher(s) who claimed that art was an imitation of nature was(were)
    I. Kant
    II. Aristotle
    III. Dewey
    IV. Augustine
    V. Santayana

    The CORRECT answer is:

    A. I *only*   B. I, III
    C. II *only*   D. I, IV, V
    E. IV, V

17. Throughout the Middle Ages, art was
    I. held in philosophical disrespect
    II. irrelevant to religion
    III. designed to portray religious sentiments
    IV. banned entirely
    V. used to encourage moral behavior

    The CORRECT answer is:

    A. I *only*   B. I, II
    C. III *only*   D. IV *only*
    E. III, V

18. The philosopher(s) who claimed that the purpose of art is to give pleasure was(were)
    I. Plato
    II. Aristotle
    III. Santayana
    IV. Kant
    V. Dewey
    The CORRECT answer is:

    A. I only
    B. I, IV
    C. III only
    D. IV only
    E. II, V

19. The philosopher(s) who claimed that art concerns the character of humans was(were)
    I. Plato
    II. Aristotle
    III. Santayana
    IV. Kant
    V. Dewey
    The CORRECT answer is:

    A. I only
    B. I, III
    C. II only
    D. I, IV, V
    E. V only

20. The philosopher(s) who thought that art should have social significance was(were)
    I. Plato
    II. Aristotle
    III. Santayana
    IV. Kant
    V. Dewey
    The CORRECT answer is:

    A. I only
    B. II, V
    C. III only
    D. V only
    E. IV, V

21. The philosopher(s) who thought that the most beautiful art symbolized moral goodness was(were)
    I. Plato
    II. Aristotle
    III. Santayana
    IV. Kant
    V. Dewey
    The CORRECT answer is:

    A. I only
    B. II, V
    C. III only
    D. IV only
    E. I, III, V

22. According to the philosopher Schopenhauer, art is *primarily*
    I. a means to a moral end
    II. aimed at social significance
    III. used as an escape
    IV. designed to make people better citizens
    V. a reflection of nature
    The CORRECT answer is:

    A. I *only*
    B. I, IV
    C. II *only*
    D. III *only*
    E. I, III, V

23. Benedetto Croce, the aesthetician, believed that art is
    I. therapeutic
    II. an enrichment of everyday life
    III. found in normal, everyday experiences
    IV. an intuition of ultimate reality
    V. spiritual
    The CORRECT answer is:

    A. I *only*
    B. I, III
    C. II, III
    D. IV *only*
    E. IV, V

24. The only philosopher to suggest that art be banned in society is

    A. Plato
    B. Aristotle
    C. Dewey
    D. Santayana
    E. Croce

25. Among other philosophers and thinkers, the one(s) who believe that religious devotion is based *primarily* upon human reason is(are)
    I. Luther
    II. Calvin
    III. Kant
    IV. Nietzsche
    V. Kierkegaard
    The CORRECT answer is:

    A. I *only*
    B. II *only*
    C. I, II
    D. III *only*
    E. IV, V

26. Cosraological arguments for the existence of God are *primarily* based on
    I. faith
    II. reason
    III. nature
    IV. God's will
    V. a priori logic
    The CORRECT answer is:

    A. I *only*
    B. I, IV
    C. II, V
    D. III *only*
    E. I, III, V

27. Ontological arguments for the existence of God are *primarily* based on
    I. faith
    II. reason
    III. nature
    IV. God's will
    V. a priori logic
    The CORRECT answer is:

    A. I *only*
    B. I, IV
    C. II, V
    D. III *only*
    E. I, III, V

28. Teleological arguments for the existence of God are *primarily* based on
    I. divine revelation
    II. faith
    III. reason
    IV. the design of nature
    V. a priori logic
    The CORRECT answer is:

    A. I *only*
    B. I, II
    C. III, V
    D. IV *only*
    E. I, II, V

29. The claim that God is *omniscient* means that He is

    A. without a beginning or an end
    B. all-powerful
    C. everywhere at all times
    D. all-knowing
    E. the source of grace

30. The claim that God is *omnipresent* means that He is
    I. without a beginning or an end
    II. all-powerful
    III. everywhere at all times
    IV. all-knowing
    V. the source of grace
    The CORRECT answer is:

    A. I *only*
    B. II *only*
    C. I, IV
    D. III *only*
    E. V *only*

31. The claim that God is *omnipotent* means that He is
    I. without a beginning or an end
    II. all-powerful
    III. everywhere at all times
    IV. all-knowing
    V. the source of grace
    The CORRECT answer is:

    A. I *only*
    B. I, III
    C. II *only*
    D. IV *only*
    E. IV, V

32. The claim that no one can deserve to go to Heaven indicates that God is
    I. without a beginning or an end
    II. all-powerful
    III. everywhere at all times
    IV. all-knowing
    V. the source of grace
    The CORRECT answer is:

    A. I only
    B. I, III
    C. II, IV
    D. IV only
    E. V only

33. One problem concerning God's infinite goodness is that
    I. no one has ever seen God
    II. Jesus spoke in vague parables
    III. there is so much evil in the world
    IV. people have no free will
    V. disasters like the Holocaust increase religious skepticism
    The CORRECT answer is:

    A. I only
    B. I, II
    C. III only
    D. III, V
    E. I, III, V

34. The thinker and philosopher Siddhartha Gautama founded the religion of

    A. Hinduism
    B. Buddhism
    C. Taoism
    D. Confucianism
    E. Theism

35. The Buddha was a thinker, teacher and philosopher who
    I. was born poor and humble
    II. was born rich and powerful
    III. advocated rejecting desires
    IV. denied the existence of the self
    V. claimed that God resides in the self
    The CORRECT answer is:

    A. I only
    B. I, V
    C. II, V
    D. II, III
    E. II, III, IV

36. Buddha claimed that the ultimate goal of every human being is to
    I. live the most pleasurable life
    II. attain Nirvana
    III. reject all pleasures of life
    IV. use moderation in all activities
    V. worship God
    The CORRECT answer is:

    A. I only
    B. I, V
    C. II, III
    D. II, IV
    E. II, V

37. A *primary* concept in Judaism is
    I. the grace of God
    II. the covenant
    III. God's infinite love
    IV. the law of God
    V. revelation
    The CORRECT answer is:

    A. I, V
    B. II *only*
    C. II, IV
    D. II, III
    E. III, V

38. Fundamental concepts in Catholicism are
    I. the law of God
    II. God's divinity in Christ
    III. the Trinity
    IV. revelation
    V. sacraments
    The CORRECT answer is:

    A. I *only*
    B. I, III
    C. II, III, IV
    D. II, III, V
    E. I, V

39. The religion of Islam is based on
    I. the Koran
    II. an afterlife of spiritual existence
    III. the prophet Mohammed
    IV. God's infinite mercy
    V. a Heaven full of sensual pleasures
    The CORRECT answer is:

    A. I *only*
    B. I, II
    C. I, III
    D. II, IV
    E. I, III, V

40. Protestantism focuses *primarily* upon
    I. individual dignity
    II. a personal God
    III. sacraments
    IV. intermediaries between man and God
    V. attaining moral behavior based on Christ's teachings
    The CORRECT answer is:

    A. I *only*
    B. II, III
    C. I, II, IV
    D. I, II, V
    E. I, III, IV

41. The *primary* problem with the claim "an act such as murder is wrong because God says it is," is that
    I. some people think murder is right
    II. it is difficult to know what God says
    III. morality can be observed independently of God's word
    IV. atheists cannot be moral
    V. religious people must use extreme self-discipline to avoid sin
    The CORRECT answer is:

    A. I, III
    B. II *only*
    C. II, IV
    D. III, V
    E. III, IV, V

42. The problem with the claim, "God says that murder is wrong because it is," is that
    I. some people think murder is right
    II. it is difficult to know what God says
    III. morality can be observed independently of God's word
    IV. atheists cannot be moral
    V. religious people must use extreme self-discipline to avoid sin
    The CORRECT answer is:

    A. I *only*
    B. I, II
    C. III *only*
    D. II, IV
    E. I, III, V

43. Claim A: "Murder is wrong because God says it is." Claim B: "God says murder is wrong because it is."
    The logical result of believing *either* Claim A or Claim B is that
    I. some people think murder is right
    II. it is difficult to know what God says
    III. morality is logically independent of God's word
    IV. atheists can be moral
    V. religious people must use extreme self-discipline not to sin
    The CORRECT answer is:

    A. I *only*
    B. I, V
    C. II, IV
    D. III, IV
    E. II, IV, V

44. The philosopher(s) who claimed that religion was the opiate of the people is(are)
    I. Aristotle
    II. Plato
    III. Marx
    IV. Hegel
    V. Kierkegaard
    The CORRECT answer is:

    A. I *only*
    B. I, V
    C. I, III
    D. III *only*
    E. V *only*

45. *Individualism* is a theory that is MOST incompatible with the philosophy of
    I. Aristotle
    II. John Stuart Mill
    III. Jeremy Bentham
    IV. Karl Marx
    V. Nietzsche
    The CORRECT answer is:

    A. I *only*
    B. I, II
    C. II, III
    D. I, IV
    E. IV, V

46. *Organicism* is a theory of society that claims that
    I. individuals make up the primary component of societies
    II. societies are whole entities
    III. the whole of society is greater than the sum of its parts
    IV. humans are mutually independent of each other
    V. humans are mutually dependent on each other
    The CORRECT answer is:

    A. I *only*
    B. I, IV
    C. II, III
    D. II, III, IV
    E. II, III, V

47. The philosopher(s) who believed that society should be classless is(are)
    I. Aristotle
    II. Plato
    III. John Stuart Mill
    IV. Karl Marx
    V. Machiavelli
    The CORRECT answer is:

    A. I *only*
    B. II *only*
    C. I, III
    D. II, IV
    E. II, III, V

48. The philosopher(s) who believed that society should be ruled democratically is(are)
    I. Aristotle
    II. Plato
    III. John Stuart Mill
    IV. Hobbes
    V. Machiavelli
    The CORRECT answer is:

    A. I *only*
    B. I, II
    C. II, IV
    D. III *only*
    E. III, IV, V

49. The philosopher(s) who believed that society ought to have an absolute monarch is(are)
    I. Aristotle
    II. Plato
    III. Hobbes
    IV. Machiavelli
    V. Luther
    The CORRECT answer is:

    A. I *only*
    B. I, II
    C. II, IV
    D. III, IV
    E. III, IV, V

50. St. Thomas Aquinas' political philosophy emphasized
    I. an egoist human nature
    II. natural law
    III. predestination
    IV. free will
    V. absolute rule
    The CORRECT answer is:

    A. I, V
    B. II, III
    C. II, IV
    D. I, III
    E. I, III, V

KEY (CORRECT ANSWERS)

1. E	11. C	21. D	31. C	41. C
2. C	12. D	22. D	32. E	42. C
3. D	13. D	23. E	33. D	43. D
4. C	14. D	24. A	34. B	44. D
5. D	15. B	25. D	35. E	45. D
6. C	16. C	26. D	36. D	46. E
7. B	17. E	27. C	37. C	47. D
8. C	18. C	28. D	38. D	48. D
9. D	19. C	29. D	39. E	49. E
10. C	20. D	30. D	40. D	50. C

TEST 2

DIRECTIONS: Each question or incomplete statement is followed by several suggested answers or completions. Select the one that BEST answers the question or completes the statement. *PRINT THE LETTER OF THE CORRECT ANSWER IN THE SPACE AT THE RIGHT.*

1. Machiavelli's political philosophy emphasized that 1.____
    I. the people know what is best for them
    II. rulers ought to appear just, but not really be just
    III. rulers who are just are the most successful
    IV. moral insight and sensitivity are more important than prudence
    V. ruling a society is based on strength and cunning
   The CORRECT answer is:

   A. I only   B. I, IV
   C. II, III   D. II, V
   E. I, II, IV

2. Terms associated with Machiavelli's political philosophy are 2.____
    I. morality
    II. glory
    III. self-interest
    IV. prudence
    V. power
   The CORRECT answer is:

   A. I, III   B. II, V
   C. II, III, V   D. III, V
   E. II, III, IV, V

3. Terms associated with Hobbes' political philosophy are 3.____
    I. morality
    II. glory
    III. self-interest
    IV. contract
    V. power
   The CORRECT answer is:

   A. I only   B. I, IV
   C. II, III   D. III, IV
   E. II, IV, V

4. *Theocracy* is a system of government in which _____ rule. 4.____
    I. aristocrats
    II. landowners
    III. rich people
    IV. the people
    V. religious leaders
   The CORRECT answer is:

   A. I only   B. I, IV
   C. III, V   D. II, III
   E. V only

55

5. Philosophers advocating a version of Social Contract Theory are
    I. Machiavelli
    II. Plato
    III. Hobbes
    IV. Locke
    V. Mill

    The CORRECT answer is:

    A. I only
    B. I, III
    C. II, V
    D. III, IV
    E. II, IV, V

6. Philosophers who argued AGAINST a political philosophy based on contract theory are
    I. Plato
    II. Hobbes
    III. Mill
    IV. Rousseau
    V. Marx

    The CORRECT answer is:

    A. I, III
    B. II only
    C. II, IV
    D. I, III, IV
    E. I, III, V

7. Philosophers who based their political philosophies upon a "state of nature" are
    I. Plato
    II. Locke
    III. Hobbes
    IV. Mill
    V. Rousseau

    The CORRECT answer is:

    A. I, II
    B. II, IV
    C. II, III, V
    D. I, III, IV
    E. II, IV, V

8. Philosophers who postulate sociable and moral human beings in the state of nature are
    I. Plato
    II. Locke
    III. Hobbes
    IV. Mill
    V. Rousseau

    The CORRECT answer is:

    A. I, II
    B. II, V
    C. I, III, IV
    D. II, IV
    E. II, IV, V

9. The political philosopher(s) credited with originating universal ethical egoism is(are)
    I. Aristotle
    II. Hobbes
    III. Locke
    IV. John Stuart Mill
    V. Karl Marx
   The CORRECT answer is:

   A. I only
   B. II only
   C. III only
   D. IV only
   E. III, IV, V

10. The political philosopher(s) for whom the consent of the people is important is(are)
    I. Plato
    II. Hobbes
    III. Mill
    IV. Locke
    V. Marx
   The CORRECT answer is:

   A. I only
   B. I, V
   C. II, III
   D. IV, V
   E. V only

11. Advocates of rule by aristocracy include
    I. Burke and Paine
    II. Aristotle and Burke
    III. Plato and Luther
    IV. Plato and Calvin
    V. Burke and Calvin
   The CORRECT answer is:

   A. I only
   B. II only
   C. I, IV
   D. II, III
   E. II, V

12. The political philosopher(s) who believed that the sovereign provides SOLE support for social stability is(are)
    I. Plato
    II. Marx
    III. John Stuart Mill
    IV. Rousseau
    V. Hobbes
   The CORRECT answer is:

   A. I only
   B. I, III
   C. IV only
   D. II, III, IV
   E. V only

13. The political philosopher(s) credited with instituting natural rights of life, liberty and the protection of property is(are)
    I. Aquinas
    II. Rousseau
    III. Locke
    IV. Hobbes
    V. John Stuart Mill
    The CORRECT answer is:

    A. I only
    B. I, II
    C. III only
    D. IV only
    E. III, IV, V

14. The philosopher(s) who advocated disobedience to a sovereign who failed to protect the country from outside attack or to enforce contracts is(are)
    I. Rousseau
    II. Locke
    III. Jeremy Bentham
    IV. Hobbes
    V. Karl Marx
    The CORRECT answer is:

    A. I, IV
    B. IV only
    C. III, IV
    D. II, V
    E. V only

15. The political philosopher(s) famous for basing proper government upon the "general will" is(are)
    I. Rousseau
    II. Locke
    III. Hobbes
    IV. Jeremy Bentham
    V. Karl Marx
    The CORRECT answer is:

    A. I only
    B. I, II
    C. II, III
    D. III
    E. IV, V

16. The political philosopher(s) credited for originating liberalism is(are)
    I. Plato
    II. Marx
    III. Bentham
    IV. John Stuart Mill
    V. Spinoza
    The CORRECT answer is:

    A. I only
    B. I, V
    C. II, III
    D. III, IV
    E. III, V

17. MAIN doctrines of Karl Marx's political philosophy include
    I. individual sovereignty
    II. general will
    III. natural rights
    IV. economic determinism
    V. representative democracy
    The CORRECT answer is:

    A. I, V
    B. II, III
    C. IV only
    D. III only
    E. IV, V

18. The *primary* obstacle(s) to social justice, according to Marx, is(are)
    I. wealth
    II. private property
    III. abundant labor
    IV. scarce labor
    V. poverty
    The CORRECT answer is:

    A. I *only*
    B. II *only*
    C. I, III
    D. II, IV
    E. V *only*

19. Karl Marx's political philosophy is BEST described as
    I. dialectical idealism
    II. material eclecticism
    III. materialistic representation
    IV. historical materialism
    V. dialectical materialism
    The CORRECT answer is:

    A. I *only*
    B. II, III
    C. IV *only*
    D. IV, V
    E. II, IV

20. The historical precedent(s) for the American Bill of Rights was(were)
    I. Jeremy Bentham's hedonistic calculus
    II. John Stuart Mill's version of utilitarianism
    III. the 1689 English Bill of Rights
    IV. Rousseau's Social Contract Theory
    V. John Locke's natural rights theory
    The CORRECT answer is:

    A. I *only*
    B. II, IV
    C. III *only*
    D. IV, V
    E. V *only*

21. Thomas Jefferson borrowed *primarily* from the thoughts of the political philosopher

    A. Jeremy Bentham
    B. John Stuart Mill
    C. Jean-Jacques Rousseau
    D. John Locke
    E. Thomas Hobbes

22. The *primary* provision(s) of a Writ of Habeas Corpus is(are)
    I. a jury trial
    II. a trial by one's peers
    III. to protect citizens during civil war
    IV. to inform the accused of the charges against him
    V. to avoid retractive legislation
    The CORRECT answer is:

    A. I *only*   B. I, II
    C. II, IV   D. III, V
    E. IV *only*

23. The Bill of Rights in the United States is
    I. the first ten amendments to the Constitution
    II. the last ten amendments to the Constitution
    III. a direct result of Locke's political philosophy
    IV. derived from Rousseau's general will doctrine
    V. designed to protect citizens from the government
    The CORRECT answer is:

    A. I, III   B. II, IV
    C. I, III, IV   D. I, III, V
    E. II, III, IV

24. Of the several ideas developed by John Locke, our Declaration of Independence includes
    I. the right to bear arms
    II. equality of all human beings
    III. rights to property
    IV. the pursuit of happiness
    V. governmental obligation to protect citizens
    The CORRECT answer is:

    A. I, III   B. II *only*
    C. II, III, IV   D. I, IV, V
    E. II, III, IV, V

25. The philosopher(s) who developed a theory of history include(s)
    I. Plato
    II. Vico
    III. Rousseau
    IV. Marx
    V. Hegel
    The CORRECT answer is:

    A. I *only*   B. I, II
    C. II, III, V   D. II, IV, V
    E. I, III, V

26. The philosopher(s) who believed that history is *primarily* the result of reason is(are)   26._____
    I. Aristotle
    II. Kant
    III. Marx
    IV. Hegel
    V. Plato
    The CORRECT answer is:

    A. I, V   B. II, IV
    C. III *only*   D. II, III
    E. II, IV, V

27. The philosopher(s) whose theories are *dialectical* include   27._____
    I. Plato
    II. Aristotle
    III. Hegel
    IV. Marx
    V. Locke
    The CORRECT answer is:

    A. I *only*   B. I, II
    C. II, III, IV   D. I, III, IV
    E. II, IV, V

28. The famous "Master-Slave Paradox" originated from the political philosophy of   28._____
    I. Aristotle
    II. Plato
    III. Rousseau
    IV. Marx
    V. Hegel
    The CORRECT answer is:

    A. I, III   B. II, IV
    C. III *only*   D. IV *only*
    E. V *only*

29. The philosopher(s) whose theories are a direct reaction against Kant's is(are)   29._____
    I. Hegel
    II. Rousseau
    III. Nietzsche
    IV. Kierkegaard
    V. Sartre
    The CORRECT answer is:

    A. I *only*   B. I, III
    C. III, IV   D. III, V
    E. III, IV, V

30. The philosopher(s) who considered aesthetics to triumph over morality was(were)
    I. Plato
    II. Aristotle
    III. Kant
    IV. Nietzsche
    V. Mill
    The CORRECT answer is:

    A. I only
    B. I, III
    C. II, IV
    D. IV only
    E. IV, V

31. Friedrich Nietzsche authored
    I. "The Fear and Trembling"
    II. "The Genealogy of Morals"
    III. "The Sickness Unto Death"
    IV. "The Birth of Tragedy"
    V. "The Critique of Pure Reason"
    The CORRECT answer is:

    A. I only
    B. I, III
    C. II, IV
    D. II, V
    E. V only

32. "Hedonism" differs from "Eudaemonism" in that the former means _____ while the latter means _____.

    A. self-control; happiness
    B. happiness; pleasure
    C. pleasure; happiness
    D. pleasure; asceticism
    E. happiness; self-control

33. The philosophy of Francis Bacon
    I. formed the substance of modern science
    II. relied primarily upon common sense
    III. emphasized critical observation
    IV. rejected ultimate causes
    V. followed closely upon Plato's
    The CORRECT answer is:

    A. I only
    B. I, V
    C. I, II, IV
    D. I, III, V
    E. I, III, IV

34. The philosopher(s) who largely contributed to the rise of modern science is(are)
    I. Hume
    II. Locke
    III. Kant
    IV. Rousseau
    V. Bacon
    The CORRECT answer is:

    A. I only
    B. I, III
    C. I, II, IV
    D. I, II, V
    E. I, II, III

35. The philosophical school of *logical empiricism* includes the philosophers
    I. James
    II. Wittgenstein
    III. Dewey
    IV. Russell
    V. Carnap
    The CORRECT answer is:

    A. I, III
    B. II, IV
    C. II, IV, V
    D. III, IV
    E. I, IV, V

36. A MAJOR division of philosophical schools in the modern era can be characterized as that between
    I. reason and emotion
    II. idealism and materialism
    III. analytical and continental
    IV. rational and existentialist
    V. idealism and analytical
    The CORRECT answer is:

    A. I only
    B. I, II
    C. I, III
    D. I, III, IV
    E. I, III, V

37. The philosopher Lucretius wrote
    I. "The Organon"
    II. "On the Nature of Things"
    III. "The Enneads"
    IV. "The Meditations"
    V. "The Nichomachean Ethics"
    The CORRECT answer is:

    A. I only
    B. I, V
    C. II only
    D. III only
    E. III, IV

38. Aristotle did NOT author
    I. "The Organon"
    II. "The Poetics"
    III. "The Phaedo"
    IV. "The Nichomachean Ethics"
    V. "The Monologium"
    The CORRECT answer is:

    A. I, III
    B. II, IV
    C. III only
    D. III, V
    E. II, III, V

39. The author of the "Prolegomena to any Future Metaphysics" was

    A. Spinoza
    B. Kant
    C. Descartes
    D. Hegel
    E. Rousseau

40. John Stuart Mill authored
    I. "The Leviathan"
    II. "Utilitarianism"
    III. "An Introduction to the Principles of Morals and Legislation"
    IV. "On Liberty"
    V. "The Social Contract"
    The CORRECT answer is:

    A. I only
    B. II only
    C. I, III
    D. II, IV
    E. II, IV, V

41. The philosopher(s) who invented logical paradoxes is(are)
    I. Zeno
    II. Plato
    III. Aristotle
    IV. Buridan
    V. Mill
    The CORRECT answer is:

    A. I only
    B. II, III
    C. I, IV
    D. III, V
    E. V only

42. Assumptions of modern game theory, used in moral and political philosophy, are
    I. irrationality
    II. rationality
    III. choice
    IV. maximization
    V. non-cooperation
    The CORRECT answer is:

    A. I, III
    B. II, IV
    C. II, III, V
    D. II, III, IV, V
    E. All of the above

43. The existentialist philosopher(s) who was(were) also Marxist is(are)
    I. Sartre
    II. Kierkegaard
    III. Nietzsche
    IV. Camus
    V. Marcel
    The CORRECT answer is:

    A. I only
    B. II, III
    C. III only
    D. IV, V
    E. V only

44. The existentialist philosopher(s) who was(were) NOT atheist is(are)
    I. Sartre
    II. Kierkegaard
    III. Nietzsche
    IV. Camus
    V. Marcel
    The CORRECT answer is:

    A. I *only*
    B. I, III
    C. II *only*
    D. II, IV
    E. II, V

45. The BEST way to characterize individualist social theory, as opposed to collectivist theory, is that on the
    I. former, individuals are mutually interdependent
    II. former, individuals are not mutually interdependent
    III. latter, the whole is equal to the sum of its parts
    IV. latter, the whole is more than the sum of its parts
    V. former, the whole is more than the sum of its parts
    The CORRECT answer is:

    A. I *only*
    B. I, III
    C. II, IV
    D. I, III, V
    E. II, III

46. *Collectivists* in political philosophy include
    I. Plato
    II. Mill
    III. Hobbes
    IV. Aristotle
    V. Marx
    The CORRECT answer is:

    A. I *only*
    B. V *only*
    C. II, IV
    D. I, IV
    E. I, IV, V

47. The difference between *intrinsic* and *extrinsic* good is that
    I. the former is not attainable
    II. the former leads to nothing more
    III. the latter leads to nothing more
    IV. only one has been the object of philosophical scrutiny
    V. one is a means and the other is an end
    The CORRECT answer is:

    A. I *only*
    B. I, IV
    C. II, V
    D. III, IV
    E. I, III, V

48. The philosopher(s) who believed that friends, money and social status are important include
    I. Plato
    II. Aristotle
    III. Descartes
    IV. John Stuart Mill
    V. Marx
    The CORRECT answer is:

    A. I only
    B. II only
    C. I, III
    D. II, V
    E. II, IV, V

49. The term "teleological" comes from the Greek word "telos" meaning
    I. love
    II. purpose
    III. goal
    IV. logic
    V. reason
    The CORRECT answer is:

    A. I only
    B. I, II
    C. II, III
    D. I, IV, V
    E. V only

50. According to Aristotle, a morally good person is one who
    I. contemplates universal virtues
    II. follows in Plato's path
    III. leads an active and athletic life
    IV. is healthy and good-looking
    V. develops deliberate habits
    The CORRECT answer is:

    A. I
    B. I, II
    C. III, V
    D. III, IV
    E. III, IV, V

KEY (CORRECT ANSWERS)

1. D	11. E	21. D	31. C	41. C
2. E	12. E	22. E	32. D	42. E
3. D	13. C	23. D	33. E	43. A
4. E	14. B	24. E	34. D	44. E
5. D	15. A	25. D	35. C	45. C
6. E	16. D	26. B	36. D	46. E
7. C	17. C	27. D	37. C	47. C
8. B	18. B	28. E	38. D	48. E
9. B	19. D	29. E	39. B	49. C
10. D	20. C	30. D	40. D	50. E

EXAMINATION SECTION
TEST 1

DIRECTIONS: Each question or incomplete statement is followed by several suggested answers or completions. Select the one that BEST answers the question or completes the statement. *PRINT THE LETTER OF THE CORRECT ANSWER IN THE SPACE AT THE RIGHT.*

1. The term "philosophy" literally means

    A. abstract thinking
    B. love of wisdom
    C. speculative conjecture
    D. profound thought
    E. study of the human mind

    1._____

2. Plato was the student of

    A. Aristotle
    B. Epictetus
    C. Homer
    D. Sophocles
    E. Socrates

    2._____

3. Which of the following people did NOT discuss justice with Socrates in THE REPUBLIC?

    A. Glaucon
    B. Thrasymachus
    C. Epictetus
    D. Adeimantos
    E. Polemarchos

    3._____

4. Epistemology is

    A. the Greek notion of excellence
    B. the study of ultimate reality
    C. the philosophy of language
    D. the theory of knowledge
    E. theology

    4._____

5. In the CRITO, Plato reports that Socrates chose to stay in jail because

    A. Crito came too late
    B. Crito never spoke to Socrates
    C. Crito's argument was weak
    D. Plato did not pay the fine
    E. none of the above

    5._____

6. Karl Marx, in his political theory, maintains that

    A. ideas are greatly dependent on economic conditions
    B. man is primarily a physical being
    C. belief in God is unfounded
    D. alienation is an effect of capitalism
    E. all of the above

    6._____

7. Which philosopher maintained that we need to make a "leap of faith" to believe in God?

    A. Descartes
    B. St. Anselm
    C. Kierkegaard
    D. Kant
    E. Thomas Aquinas

    7._____

8. The idea that God is the prime mover is associated with

   A. William James
   B. Karl Marx
   C. The Logical Positivists
   D. Aquinas
   E. two of the above

9. St. Anselm's argument for the existence of God contends that

   A. an examination of the universe confirms that God exists
   B. only priests can know for certain that God exists
   C. God's existence is only proved scientifically
   D. God's existence is entailed in the concept of "God"
   E. none of the above

10. Empiricism supports the view that

    A. there are innate ideas
    B. knowledge is unrelated to sense experience
    C. sense experience is the primary source of knowledge
    D. mysticism is the best way to know the world
    E. none of the above

11. The ontological argument maintains that the idea of a nonexistent God is

    A. self-contradictory
    B. the belief of fools
    C. impious and heretical
    D. a consequence of not paying attention to the universe
    E. the work of the devil

12. The cosmological argument seeks to establish that

    A. the notion of God has little value
    B. God exists only in the mind of the believer
    C. the universe is the cause of God
    D. the universe and God are not related
    E. God is the cause of the universe

13. *A priori* and *a posteriori* are distinctions that refer to

    A. only ethical beliefs
    B. types of political theories
    C. the belief in God
    D. the philosophical contributions of Kant alone
    E. none of the above

14. Medieval philosophy is characterized by
    I. a great spirit of empirical research
    II. a rejection of empirical research
    III. a rejection of theology
    IV. a conviction that faith and reason are mutually exclusive
    V. theological questions
    The CORRECT answer is:

A. I, III
B. II, III
C. II, IV, V
D. III, IV, V
E. all of the above

15. The Ontological Argument was advanced by
    I. Schopenhauer
    II. Nietzsche
    III. St. Anselm of Canterbury
    IV. Marcus Aurelius
    V. St. Thomas Aquinas
    The CORRECT answer is:

    A. I *only*
    B. II, III
    C. II, IV
    D. III, V
    E. II, III, IV, V

16. "Act as if your action were to become a universal law of nature" is one of the possible expressions of

    A. the categorical imperative
    B. the hypothetical imperative
    C. the principle of utility
    D. an existentialist morality
    E. none of the above

17. In general, teleological views hold that

    A. acts are worthwhile only if done from a sense of duty
    B. happiness is never pursued as a moral value
    C. in ethics and science, matters can be understood in terms of their internal mechanisms
    D. in ethics and science, matters can be understood in terms of their end result or purpose
    E. none of the above

18. According to the concept of freedom found in Mill's ON LIBERTY,

    A. the government should take an active role in redistributing income
    B. the only grounds for interfering in the lives of adults is to prevent harm to others
    C. men are equal only before the sight of God
    D. because of historical changes, some men are justified in claiming greater liberty than others
    E. all of the above

19. The categorical imperative states an ethical norm that
    I. depends on certain sociological conditions
    II. applies only when the person is interested in happiness
    III. is derived from reason alone
    IV. is universally valid
    V. is only applicable in cases of emergency
    The CORRECT answer is:

    A. I, II
    B. I, III
    C. II, III, IV
    D. III, IV
    E. I, IV, V

20. John Locke believed that human beings were

    A. born without rights
    B. born with some rights which could be taken from them
    C. born with inalienable rights
    D. given their rights by society
    E. able to earn their rights by obeying the laws of the state

21. A philosophical method called "methodological doubt" is associated with the philosophy of

    A. Plato   B. Aristotle
    C. Descartes   D. William James
    E. none of the above

22. Epistemology is a philosophical concern whose *main* interest is the clarification of problems related to

    A. moral values
    B. the nature and sources of knowledge
    C. the essence of the prime mover
    D. different logical questions
    E. a system of Eastern philosophy

23. Descartes reached the statement "I think, therefore I am" as a

    A. conclusion of his views of the solar system
    B. direct consequence of his own geometrical system
    C. conclusion of his methodological doubt
    D. direct consequence of his doubts about religion
    E. none of the above

24. Locke's concept of a "tabula rasa" (blank slate) states that the mind is

    A. born with innate ideas
    B. never able to know any truths
    C. able to understand the nature of God
    D. born with no innate ideas
    E. able to be reincarnated in animals

25. In the "Myth of the Cave," from Plato's REPUBLIC, the idea of the Good is symbolized by the

    A. cave itself   B. fire in the cave
    C. sun   D. shadows
    E. all of the above

26. In Plato's theory of value,

    A. values are dependent on personal preference
    B. man is the measure of all things
    C. it all depends upon where you were born
    D. there is a transcendent form of good
    E. sense experience is the key to the highest good

27. The Delphi Oracle was

   A. a philosophical system
   B. a contribution of the Milesian rationalists
   C. a figment of Plato's imagination
   D. a Greek religious institution
   E. one of Plato's dialogues

28. Greek Atomism was a system of cosmology developed by

   A. Aristotle   B. Democritus
   C. Marcus Aurelius   D. Thales
   E. none of the above

29. Cosmology is the study of the

   A. cosmos
   B. origin of the universe
   C. nature of the end of the world
   D. ultimate principles of reality
   E. all of the above

30. In "The Apology," Socrates *affirms* his

   A. support of atomism
   B. denial of life after death
   C. uncertainty about what death entails
   D. rejection of religion
   E. none of the above

31. *Platonism* is a philosophical style characterized by a(n)

   A. conviction that sense experience is primary
   B. denial of the possibility of knowledge
   C. contempt for mathematics
   D. affirmation of atomism
   E. rejection of sense experience

32. At his trial, Socrates was charged with

   A. a misuse of political power
   B. neglecting his military duties
   C. squandering public finances
   D. believing that water was the ultimate element
   E. corrupting the young

33. Pascal's Wager was a bet Pascal made

   A. with God
   B. with the devil
   C. concerning whether or not he should believe in God
   D. concerning whether or not he should live a virtuous life
   E. none of the above

34. The philosopher who wrote "Crito", "Phaedo", and "The Symposium" was

   A. Socrates
   B. Aeschylus
   C. Heraclitus
   D. Democritus
   E. none of the above

35. *Ethical absolutism* claims that
   I. when in Rome, do as the Romans do
   II. if something is wrong, it is always wrong
   III. if something is right, it is always right
   IV. right actions do not vary from culture to culture
   V. all of the above
   The CORRECT answer is:

   A. I *only*
   B. II *only*
   C. II, III
   D. II, III, IV
   E. V *only*

36. *Aesthetics* is that branch of philosophy that deals with

   A. theological disputes
   B. relativism in ethics
   C. the nature of knowledge
   D. the nature of reality
   E. the nature of beauty

37. A person who claims to be an *agnostic* is one who doesn't know

   A. what he/she is talking about
   B. how to determine truth
   C. whether or not God exists
   D. whether or not anyone has knowledge
   E. none of the above

38. An *atheist* is one who believes that

   A. no one can know whether or not there is a God
   B. there is a God
   C. there is no God
   D. it is irrelevant whether or not there is a God
   E. philosophical knowledge is impossible

39. Algebra was invented by the philosopher

   A. Maimonides
   B. Aristotle
   C. Plato
   D. Descartes
   E. Hobbes

40. *Altruism* is the view that states

   A. no one does anything for another person, only for himself
   B. everyone does things for others, occasionally
   C. sometimes some people do things to benefit another
   D. everyone acts only out of self-interest
   E. helping others is bound to hurt yourself

41. A philosopher who argued persuasively AGAINST real altruism was   41._____

    A. Plato   B. Aristotle
    C. Kant   D. Bentham
    E. Hobbes

42. An *analogy* is a   42._____

    A. strange analysis revealing a hidden premise
    B. simile
    C. metaphor
    D. comparison proving a point
    E. none of the above

43. Analogies were a favorite technique of   43._____

    A. Plato   B. Aristotle
    C. Kant   D. Nietzsche
    E. Moses Maimonides

44. An amoral person is one who   44._____
       I. frequently commits wrong actions but doesn't know it
      II. frequently commits right actions but doesn't know it
     III. cannot tell the difference between right and wrong
      IV. should be in prison
       V. has failed to internalize moral values
    The CORRECT answer is:

    A. I, III   B. I, IV
    C. II, III   D. III, IV
    E. III, V

45. When a philosopher "analyzes" something, he   45._____

    A. determines its validity
    B. determines its soundness
    C. takes it apart to examine its consequences
    D. figures out what its consequences are
    E. assembles various views to see what combinations work

46. When a philosopher performs philosophical "synthesis" on something, he   46._____

    A. determines its validity
    B. determines its soundness
    C. takes it apart to examine its components
    D. figures out what its consequences are
    E. assembles various views to see what combinations work

47. Anarchists believe that   47._____
       I. chaos is beautiful
      II. governments are corrupt
     III. the best government is one that governs least
      IV. society can do without governments
       V. humans are by nature socially cooperative
    The CORRECT answer is:

A. I *only*   B. II
C. I, II, III   D. II, IV, V
E. III, IV, V

48. Anaximines thought the world consisted primarily of

    A. water   B. fire
    C. air   D. earth
    E. gods

49. The Pre-Socratics were philosophers who

    A. especially admired the Roman philosophers
    B. especially despised the work of Aristotle
    C. followed the paths laid out by Socrates
    D. thought a lot but wrote little down
    E. lived before Socrates

50. A skeptic is one who

    A. believes nothing
    B. believes many things but knows nothing
    C. believes many things and knows that no one knows anything
    D. believes everything
    E. knows everything

KEY (CORRECT ANSWERS)

1. B	11. A	21. C	31. E	41. E
2. E	12. E	22. B	32. E	42. D
3. C	13. E	23. C	33. D	43. A
4. D	14. C	24. D	34. E	44. E
5. C	15. D	25. C	35. D	45. C
6. E	16. A	26. D	36. E	46. E
7. C	17. D	27. D	37. C	47. D
8. D	18. B	28. B	38. C	48. C
9. D	19. D	29. B	39. D	49. E
10. C	20. C	30. C	40. C	50. B

TEST 2

DIRECTIONS: Each question or incomplete statement is followed by several suggested answers or completions. Select the one that BEST answers the question or completes the statement. *PRINT THE LETTER OF THE CORRECT ANSWER IN THE SPACE AT THE RIGHT.*

1. A *cynic* is one who believes

   A. that everything in life works out for the best
   B. that everything in life works out for the worst
   C. that hope springs eternal
   D. in very little that cannot be scientifically proven
   E. that the natural lot of man is difficulty and unhappiness

   1.____

2. *Anthropomorphism* is the view that
   I. there are many gods, not just one God
   II. no one really knows the nature of man
   III. all of nature behaves as humans do
   IV. humans lie at the center of the universe
   V. all of the above

   The CORRECT answer is:

   A. I *only*   B. II *only*
   C. II, III   D. II, IV
   E. III, IV

   2.____

3. The FIRST sign of order in the universe, according to the ancients, was

   A. mathematics   B. physics
   C. biology   D. astronomy
   E. philosophy

   3.____

4. St. Thomas became quite famous for revitalizing the views of

   A. Plato   B. Socrates
   C. Epictetus   D. Aristotle
   E. St. Anselm

   4.____

5. *Thomistic* thinking emphasizes
   I. logic and order
   II. faith and emotion
   III. the natural purposes of things
   IV. religious piety
   V. none of the above

   The CORRECT answer is:

   A. I, III   B. II, III
   C. III *only*   D. III, IV
   E. V *only*

   5.____

6. *Idealism* in philosophy is believing
    I. that we live in the best of all possible worlds
    II. that we live in the worst of all possible worlds
    III. that truth can best be found in abstraction
    IV. that truth can best be found in empirical sensation
    V. in everything that can be argued for
   The CORRECT answer is:

   A. I *only* B. III *only*
   C. III, V D. IV, V
   E. V *only*

7. Statements that offer premises and a conclusion are called

   A. conditionals B. antecedents
   C. consequents D. arguments
   E. modus ponens

8. *Asceticism* is the view that
    I. the body is an evil, though a necessary one
    II. people should have as many luxuries as possible
    III. we eat to live
    IV. we live to eat
    V. excess is a flaw in human nature
   The CORRECT answer is:

   A. I, III, V B. II, III
   C. II, IV D. III, V
   E. IV, V

9. An *autonomous* person is one who
    I. never listens to anyone else's opinions
    II. always listens to people's opinions
    III. remains independent in his/her actions
    IV. decides for himself/herself
    V. none of the above
   The CORRECT answer is:

   A. I *only* B. II *only*
   C. I, III D. II, III
   E. III, IV

10. *Axiology* is the study of

    A. bodies B. minds
    C. values D. moral principles
    E. duties

11. Philosophers who were also scientists were
    I. Aristotle St.
    II. Thomas Aquinas
    III. Sir Francis
    IV. Bacon Socrates
    V. Sir Isaac Newton
   The CORRECT answer is:

A. I, II B. I, III
C. II, IV D. III, IV
E. III, V

12. The view that states that *only* sensory experience can confirm the existence of something is
    I. idealism
    II. materialism
    III. empiricism
    IV. verificationism
    V. none of the above
    The CORRECT answer is:

    A. I, II B. I, III, IV
    C. II, III, IV D. III, IV
    E. V *only*

13. The philosophical and psychological school of *behaviorism* is represented by
    I. Plato
    II. Socrates
    III. Skinner
    IV. Freud
    V. Watson
    The CORRECT answer is:

    A. II *only* B. III *only*
    C. III, IV D. III, V
    E. V *only*

14. The fundamental concept in the study of *ontology* is

    A. truth B. beauty
    C. justice D. being
    E. nothingness

15. The philosopher who invented the "hedonistic calculus" was

    A. John Stuart Mill B. Plato
    C. Epictetus D. Jeremy Bentham
    E. Thomas Hobbes

16. *Subjectivism* is the view that
    I. external objects are dependent upon human consciousness
    II. external objects exist independently of human consciousness
    III. all knowledge is dependent upon human consciousness
    IV. all knowledge is dependent upon empirical evidence
    V. truth is invariable
    The CORRECT answer is:

    A. I, III B. II, III
    C. II, IV D. II, IV, V
    E. III, V

17. *Objectivism* is the view that
    I. external objects are dependent upon human consciousness
    II. external objects exist independently of human consciousness
    III. all knowledge is dependent upon human consciousness
    IV. all knowledge is dependent upon empirical evidence
    V. truth is invariable

    The CORRECT answer is:

    A. I, III
    B. II, III, V
    C. II, IV, V
    D. IV, V
    E. V *only*

18. One of the MAJOR subjectivist philosophers was

    A. Hume
    B. Berkeley
    C. Hobbes
    D. Mill
    E. Bentham

19. A term that can be applied to Aristotle, Democritus, Karl Marx, David Hume, and Hobbes is

    A. idealist
    B. materialist
    C. empiricist
    D. relativist
    E. all of the above

20. The view that "the human mind is really only an illusion fostered by archaic thinking; in reality, we have only a brain" can be termed
    I. empiricist
    II. identity theory
    III. materialist
    IV. behaviorism
    V. reductionism

    The CORRECT answer is:

    A. I, II, III
    B. I, III, IV
    C. III, IV
    D. III, V
    E. all of the above

21. The famous dictum, "Esse ist percipi" (if it is seen, it exists), is attributed to

    A. Aristotle
    B. Hume
    C. Descartes
    D. Berkeley
    E. Locke

22. The view that humans have no "self," only a bundle of perceptions, is attributed to

    A. Aristotle
    B. Hobbes
    C. Rousseau
    D. Hume
    E. none of the above

23. Under capitalism,
    I. there is public ownership of the means of production
    II. there is private ownership of the means of production
    III. there is a gradual wearing away of the means of production
    IV. profits fluctuate with market prices
    V. profits do not fluctuate with market prices

    The CORRECT answer is:

A. I, III   B. II, III
C. II, V   D. III, V
E. V *only*

24. The famous phrase "Cogito ergo sum" is attributed to

    A. Plato   B. Berkeley
    C. Moses Maimonides D. Socrates
    E. Descartes

25. The one thing Descartes said he knew *for certain* was that

    A. he doubted
    B. his consciousness existed
    C. only the mind could be known to exist
    D. to doubt is to think
    E. all of the above

26. *Dualism* is the view that

    A. all things come in twos
    B. dividing by two will always yield a mathematical result
    C. humans are made up of minds and bodies
    D. humans should emphasize their spiritual side, not their physical side
    E. all of the above

27. Dualism, historically speaking, can be attributed to the powerful thinking of

    A. Aristotle   B. Plato
    C. Hume   D. Kant
    E. Descartes

28. The term *catharsis* refers to the theory that

    A. humans become more aggressive watching hostilities on stage
    B. humans become less aggressive watching hostilities on stage
    C. humans remain constantly aggressive or not aggressive regardless of what they watch on the stage
    D. no one knows what can trigger aggressiveness
    E. all of the above

29. The theory of catharsis was first presented by artists in

    A. Greece   B. Rome
    C. France   D. Germany
    E. Britain

30. According to Karl Marx, history is the story of

    A. private accumulation of wealth
    B. greed
    C. warring tribes
    D. class struggle
    E. none of the above

31. A famous Roman philosopher and artist was

   A. Plato
   B. Cicero
   C. Marcus Aurelius
   D. Maimonides
   E. none of the above

32. Hellenic, as opposed to Dionysian art, emphasizes
   I. structure and order
   II. passion and emotion
   III. delicate shadings
   IV. clear lines
   V. none of the above
   The CORRECT answer is:

   A. I, IV
   B. II, III
   C. II, IV
   D. III, IV
   E. V *only*

33. *Cognition* refers to the process of
   I. knowing
   II. believing
   III. thinking
   IV. dreaming
   V. wondering
   The CORRECT answer is:

   A. I *only*
   B. I, II
   C. I, III, V
   D. II, IV, V
   E. all of the above

34. Collectivist theories emphasize that

   A. each person is out for himself
   B. humans are much like other animals
   C. humans are too greedy and unnecessarily cruel to be like other animals
   D. humans are too cooperative and loving to be like other animals
   E. the minimum component of society is the group

35. Conscience is heavily emphasized by
   I. utilitarianism
   II. deontology
   III. existentialism
   IV. theology
   V. atheism
   The CORRECT answer is:

   A. II, III
   B. II, IV
   C. II, IV, V
   D. III, IV
   E. all of the above

36. A NECESSARY condition for *morality* is

   A. legal systems
   B. courts
   C. police
   D. choice
   E. knowledge

37. Empirical knowledge can be challenged because we are sometimes
    I. tricked by evil demons into believing what is not true
    II. deceived into thinking we are awake when we are asleep
    III. mistaken in what we think we see, as when we think the train tracks meet in the distance
    IV. confused
    V. all of the above
    The CORRECT answer is:

    A. I only
    B. II only
    C. II, III
    D. III, IV
    E. V only

38. Any philosophy, to be legitimate, should be

    A. coherent
    B. consistent
    C. falsifiable
    D. explainable
    E. all of the above

39. *Contiguity* means that two things

    A. are conspicuous
    B. are caused one by the other
    C. are caused by each other
    D. resemble each other
    E. are next to each other

40. The famous epistemological tract "Meditations" was written by

    A. Anselm
    B. Aquinas
    C. Descartes
    D. Maimonides
    E. Aristotle

41. The well-known political philosophy in THE LEVIATHAN was authored by

    A. Hume
    B. Bentham
    C. Mill
    D. Hobbes
    E. Adam Smith

42. The philosophers BEST known for studying and excelling in rhetoric are the

    A. Greeks
    B. Romans
    C. Medievals
    D. French
    E. English

43. The correspondence theory of truth claims that statements

    A. are true if they match up perfectly with reality
    B. are true if they meet empirical standards of science
    C. cannot be known to be since we don't know what's real
    D. must be true independently of reality
    E. none of the above

44. A *criterion* is a

    A. method
    B. system
    C. style
    D. standard
    E. theory

45. The CRITIQUE OF PURE REASON was written by

   A. Descartes
   B. Plato
   C. Aristotle
   D. Plotinus
   E. Kant

46. The philosopher and scientist famous for inventing evolutionary theory is

   A. Aristotle
   B. Francis Bacon
   C. Charles Darwin
   D. Isaac Newton
   E. Alfred Einstein

47. *Deductive* arguments are arguments that

   A. cannot be false
   B. must be proven mathematically
   C. do not rely upon empirical data
   D. have conclusions that are certain
   E. have conclusions that are only probable

48. *Inductive* arguments are arguments that

   A. cannot be false
   B. must be proven mathematically
   C. do not rely upon empirical data
   D. have conclusions that are certain
   E. have conclusions that are probable

49. *Determinism* is the view that
   I. physical existence admits of random events
   II. every event has a cause
   III. every effect has a cause
   IV. we are determined by our environments
   V. all of the above

   The CORRECT answer is:

   A. I, III, IV
   B. II, III, IV
   C. III, IV
   D. IV *only*
   E. V *only*

50. A *didactic* book is one that _____ the reader.

   A. disillusions
   B. teaches
   C. disgusts
   D. preaches at
   E. entertains

KEY (CORRECT ANSWERS)

1. B	11. E	21. D	31. B	41. D
2. E	12. C	22. D	32. A	42. B
3. D	13. D	23. C	33. E	43. A
4. D	14. D	24. E	34. E	44. D
5. A	15. D	25. E	35. A	45. E
6. C	16. A	26. C	36. D	46. C
7. D	17. C	27. E	37. C	47. D
8. A	18. B	28. B	38. E	48. E
9. E	19. B	29. A	39. E	49. B
10. C	20. E	30. D	40. C	50. B

EXAMINATION SECTION
TEST 1

DIRECTIONS: Each question or incomplete statement is followed by several suggested answers or completions. Select the one that BEST answers the question or completes the statement. *PRINT THE LETTER OF THE CORRECT ANSWER IN THE SPACE AT THE RIGHT.*

1. According to Karl Marx, the MOST dangerous class of society is the

    A. bourgeoisie
    B. proletariat
    C. petit-bourgeoisie
    D. working class
    E. none of the above

2. The BEST solution to capitalism's problems, according to Marx, would be

    A. the abolition of private property
    B. a return of feudalism
    C. unions
    D. legal reform
    E. none of the above

3. According to Descartes, scientific knowledge is
    I. the best kind of knowledge we are able to get
    II. the worst kind of knowledge we are able to get
    III. apt to deceive us at best
    IV. imprecise
    V. possible to doubt

    The CORRECT answer is:

    A. I only
    B. II only
    C. II, III
    D. II, IV
    E. II, III, IV, V

4. Truths that Descartes thought were respectable were ones that
    I. were clear and distinct
    II. concerned people's existence
    III. concerned his own existence
    IV. concerned math and geometry
    V. all of the above

    The CORRECT answer is:

    A. I only
    B. I, II
    C. I, IV
    D. II, IV
    E. V only

5. David Hume proved that
    I. we have no good reason to believe that causation is a true principle of science
    II. experience is our only basis for knowledge
    III. ultimately there is no reason to assume the future will resemble the past
    IV. we assume without evidence that like causes produce like effects
    V. all of the above

    The CORRECT answer is:

A. I, II   B. I, III, IV
C. II, III, IV   D. III, IV
E. V only

6. The thinkers who believed that humans by nature desire to know were
   I. Plato
   II. Aristotle
   III. Skinner
   IV. Freud
   V. all of the above
   The CORRECT answer is:
   A. I, II, III   B. I, III, IV
   C. II, IV   D. III, IV
   E. V only

7. *Ethics* is the study of
   A. principles of right conduct
   B. standards of goodness
   C. the ultimate goals of human society
   D. human happiness
   E. all of the above

8. The Greek word *polis*
   I. means group means city-state
   II. means 'political'
   III. is the root of our word 'political'
   IV. all of the above
   The CORRECT answer is:
   A. I, IV   B. II, IV
   C. III, IV   D. IV only
   E. V only

9. The Greek word *psyche*
   A. means soul
   B. means mind
   C. means wind
   D. is the root of our word 'psychology'
   E. all of the above

10. A knowledge of astronomy, studied by the earliest philosophers, gave early cultures
    A. impressive educational systems
    B. scholars who have lived down through history
    C. naval power
    D. indications of the scientific method
    E. something to write books about

11. The point of the Socratic story of the "Ring of Gyges" is to show that
    A. everyone covets expensive royal jewelry
    B. anyone who has a valuable ring will use it for status

C. anyone who could get away with it would exploit others
D. no one with the Ring of Gyges would dare to be immoral
E. all of the above

12. In an *aristocracy*, the rulers are

    A. those who want to be
    B. those with the most power
    C. those with the most wealth
    D. those with the best education
    E. all the people

13. In a *democracy*, the rulers are

    A. those who want to be
    B. those with the most power
    C. those with the most wealth
    D. those with the best education
    E. all the people

14. In an *oligarchy*, the rulers are

    A. those who want to be
    B. those with the most power
    C. those with the most wealth
    D. those with the best education
    E. all the people

15. In Plato's REPUBLIC, the rulers are

    A. men
    B. women
    C. men and women
    D. children
    E. philosophers

16. The 1600's were noteworthy for the
    I. rise in individualism
    II. rise of scientific investigation
    III. expansion of religious faith
    IV. origin of Protestantism
    V. all of the above
    The CORRECT answer is:

    A. I, II, IV
    B. II, III
    C. II, III, IV
    D. III *only*
    E. V *only*

17. An early forerunner of political philosophy was

    A. Hobbes
    B. Locke
    C. Plato
    D. Machiavelli
    E. Leibniz

18. Contract theorists include
    I. Marx
    II. Hobbes
    III. Locke
    IV. Rousseau
    V. John Stuart Mill
    The CORRECT answer is:

    A. I, II, III
    B. II, III, IV
    C. II, IV, V
    D. III, IV, V
    E. IV, V

19. The concept of free choice is *crucial* to the philosophical traditions of
    I. Thomism
    II. materialism
    III. existentialism
    IV. Kantianism
    V. none of the above
    The CORRECT answer is:

    A. I, III, IV
    B. I, IV
    C. II, III, IV
    D. III, IV
    E. V only

20. The empiricist David Hume thought that ideas were

    A. vague shadows of sensations
    B. derived from empirical data
    C. not as creative as they seem
    D. caused by physical impressions
    E. all of the above

21. Some concepts emphasized by Kant in his ethical theory were
    I. consequences
    II. motives
    III. reason
    IV. universal principles
    V. all of the above
    The CORRECT answer is:

    A. I, II, III, IV
    B. II, III, IV
    C. III
    D. IV only
    E. V only

22. THE FEAR AND TREMBLING AND THE SICKNESS UNTO DEATH was written by

    A. Sartre
    B. Camus
    C. Kierkegaard
    D. Nietzsche
    E. none of the above

23. Responsibility is a *fundamental* concept of

    A. utilitarianism
    B. Kantianism
    C. existentialism
    D. anarchism
    E. none of the above

24. When Sartre said "Man is condemned to be free," he meant that
    I. it is fun to make philosophical paradoxes
    II. whether we like it or not, we must make choices
    III. simply being born puts us in a situation of freedom
    IV. even when we choose not to be free, we are free
    V. to refuse to choose is to choose
    The CORRECT answer is:

    A. I, II
    B. II only
    C. II, III, V
    D. II, IV, V
    E. II, III, IV, V

25. The EXISTENTIALISTS believe that humans are by nature

    A. greedy and selfish
    B. loving and sociable
    C. cooperative and friendly
    D. free to make their own lives
    E. none of the above

26. THE REBEL, THE MYTH OF SISYPHUS and THE STRANGER were written by

    A. Sartre
    B. Bergmann
    C. Kierkegaard
    D. Nietzsche
    E. Camus

27. The philosophical school that believes life is irrational is

    A. rationalism
    B. idealism
    C. materialism
    D. existentialism
    E. all of the above

28. Novelists who were early precursors of existentialism are
    I. Tolstoy
    II. Camus
    III. Dostoevsky
    IV. Balzac
    V. Kafka
    The CORRECT answer is:

    A. I, III
    B. II, III
    C. II, III, V
    D. III, IV
    E. IV, V

29. *Quantitative* calculations are favored by the ethical school(s) of
    I. hedonism
    II. utilitarianism
    III. egoism
    IV. deontology
    V. all of the above
    The CORRECT answer is:

    A. I, II, III
    B. I, III, IV
    C. II, III, IV
    D. IV *only*
    E. V *only*

30. In ethics, *cognitivism* means that

   A. everyone can tell right from wrong
   B. hardly anyone can tell right from wrong
   C. knowing for certain what is right in each situation is mandatory to be a good person
   D. moral judgments are true or false
   E. all of the above

31. Happiness is the ultimate goal of
   I. hedonism
   II. utilitarianism
   III. Aristotle's teleological ethics
   IV. Plato's ethics
   V. deontology

   The CORRECT answer is:

   A. I, II, III, IV
   B. I, III, IV, V
   C. II, III, IV
   D. II, III, IV, V
   E. III, V

32. The philosophers who divided up the soul into parts were
   I. Plato
   II. Aristotle
   III. Hume
   IV. Descartes
   V. all of the above

   The CORRECT answer is:

   A. I, II
   B. I, II, III
   C. II, III
   D. II, III, IV
   E. V only

33. According to the ontological argument, God is
   I. physically real
   II. mentally real
   III. perfect
   IV. greater than which nothing can be conceived
   V. loving

   The CORRECT answer is:

   A. I only
   B. I, II, III
   C. I, III, IV
   D. III, IV
   E. III, IV, V

34. According to Socrates, in the CRITO, the *ultimate* reason why Socrates is obligated to obey his death sentence is that he

   A. loves Athens
   B. is old anyway
   C. was educated in public schools
   D. never left his country
   E. disliked bribery

35. INDUCTION is crucial to

　　A. theology　　　　　　　　　B. logic
　　C. science　　　　　　　　　　D. computer science
　　E. all of the above

36. An ALLEGORY is a

　　A. parable
　　B. story that has at least two levels of interpretation
　　C. story with symbolic characters
　　D. narrative tale designed to prove a point
　　E. all of the above

37. Twentieth century philosophy is characterized by
　　　　I. logical analysis
　　　　II. sentential calculus
　　　　III. ordinary language analysis
　　　　IV. historical research
　　　　V. all of the above
　　The CORRECT answer is:

　　A. I, III　　　　　　　　　　B. II, III
　　C. II, III, IV　　　　　　　　D. III, IV
　　E. V *only*

38. The Delphi Oracle is really

　　A. the word of God
　　B. a fortune-telling device
　　C. the reason why Socrates got into trouble
　　D. a place one can still go see in Greece
　　E. all of the above

39. *Tacit consent* is the theory in political philosophy that states that

　　A. citizens sign contracts with governments
　　B. governments have the right to ask for loyalty oaths
　　C. citizens owe allegiance to the government ruling their chosen place of abode
　　D. citizens have no right to disobey a law they believe to be unjust
　　E. everyone has the right to plead the Fifth Amendment

40. One of the MOST socially revolutionary political philosophies was

　　A. deontology　　　　　　　　B. intuitionism
　　C. utilitarianism　　　　　　　D. contract theory
　　E. Marxism

41. One of the MOST practical political philosophies for social reform was

　　A. deontology　　　　　　　　B. intuitionism
　　C. utilitarianism　　　　　　　D. contract theory
　　E. Marxism

42. One reason that the subject of pain has fascinated philosophers for so long is that
    I. everyone has experienced it
    II. there is no empirical evidence that can be conclusively offered for it
    III. it is intrinsically subjective
    IV. it is intimately involved in epistemological questions
    V. they are masochists
    The CORRECT answer is:

    A. I, III
    B. II, III, IV
    C. II, IV
    D. III, IV
    E. IV only

43. The *paradox of masochism* is that
    I. only sadists would think about masochists
    II. being mean to the masochist makes him happy
    III. being nice to the masochist makes his suffer
    IV. no one has a right to ask others to hurt them
    V. all of the above
    The CORRECT answer is:

    A. I, II
    B. I, II, III
    C. II, III
    D. II, III, IV
    E. V only

44. The *invisible hand* theory was promoted by

    A. Malthus
    B. Jeremy Bentham
    C. Karl Marx
    D. Adam Smith
    E. none of the above

45. The *first* philosopher to discuss DEMOGRAPHY was

    A. Aristotle
    B. Rousseau
    C. Hobbes
    D. Malthus
    E. none of the above

46. THE ORIGIN OF THE FAMILY, PRIVATE PROPERTY AND THE STATE was written by

    A. Rousseau
    B. Marx
    C. Locke
    D. Engels
    E. none of the above

47. According to Marxist theory, the family is
    I. the only place where individuals can feel comfortable
    II. the cellular form of class society
    III. a form of natural oppression
    IV. something to be abolished
    V. all of the above
    The CORRECT answer is:

    A. I, II
    B. II only
    C. II, III
    D. III, IV
    E. V only

48. Jurisprudence is studied in

    A. political philosophy
    B. aesthetics
    C. ethics
    D. philosophy of law
    E. none of the above

49. Rehabilitationism in theories of punishment is supported by

    A. deontology
    B. utilitarianism
    C. existentialism
    D. intuitionism
    E. none of the above

50. One MUST be a moral agent to

    A. act at all
    B. be held responsible for actions
    C. be legally culpable
    D. do ethics
    E. none of the above

KEY (CORRECT ANSWERS)

1. B	11. C	21. B	31. A	41. C
2. A	12. D	22. C	32. B	42. B
3. E	13. E	23. C	33. C	43. C
4. C	14. C	24. E	34. D	44. D
5. B	15. E	25. D	35. C	45. D
6. C	16. A	26. E	36. E	46. D
7. E	17. D	27. D	37. A	47. C
8. B	18. B	28. C	38. E	48. D
9. E	19. A	29. A	39. C	49. B
10. C	20. E	30. D	40. E	50. B

TEST 2

DIRECTIONS: Each question or incomplete statement is followed by several suggested answers or completions. Select the one that BEST answers the question or completes the statement. *PRINT THE LETTER OF THE CORRECT ANSWER IN THE SPACE AT THE RIGHT.*

1. People who are NOT moral agents include

    A. men
    B. women
    C. adults
    D. children
    E. foreigners

    1._____

2. Retribution is a theory of punishment which maintains that

    A. those who are guilty deserve to be punished
    B. punishment serves as a good example to others
    C. the best deterrent is to punish wrongdoers
    D. morality is irrelevant to legal decision-making
    E. all of the above

    2._____

3. When suicide was illegal in America, the rationale was that

    A. only stupid people would commit suicide
    B. only sick people would commit suicide
    C. no punishment could be harsh enough
    D. only God had the right to dispose of a life
    E. all of the above

    3._____

4. The McNaghten Rule stipulated that
    I. certain people would be considered legally insane
    II. certain people would be allowed to sit on juries
    III. American law would differ drastically from English common law
    IV. being amoral is considered mitigatory
    V. none of the above

    The CORRECT answer is:

    A. I, II
    B. I, II, III
    C. I, IV
    D. II, III, IV
    E. V *only*

    4._____

5. Philosophers who emphasized custom and habit are
    I. Plato
    II. Aristotle
    III. Hume
    IV. Rousseau
    V. Russell

    The CORRECT answer is:

    A. I, II, III
    B. I, II, IV
    C. II, III
    D. III *only*
    E. III, IV, V

    5._____

6. A presupposition is

   A. necessary for an argument
   B. inevitable in ordinary discussion
   C. logically suspect
   D. an assumption
   E. none of the above

7. A statement can be DISPROVED by a counter-example if it is

   A. ridiculous   B. unsupported
   C. a generalization   D. a universalization
   E. none of the above

8. Historical materialism, the political philosophy, originated with

   A. Aristotle   B. Plato
   C. Hobbes   D. Marx
   E. none of the above

9. Epicurus, the hedonist, advocated
   I. pursuing knowledge
   II. collecting material possessions
   III. eating only bread and water
   IV. praying
   V. all of the above

   The CORRECT answer is:

   A. I, III   B. I, III, IV
   C. II, III, IV   D. III *only*
   E. V

10. The philosopher who complained of the "tyranny of the majority" was

    A. Hobbes   B. Locke
    C. Mill   D. Rousseau
    E. Marx

11. The MAIN concept in utilitarianism, that of *utility,* means
    I. usefulness
    II. futility
    III. prudence
    IV. happiness
    V. pleasure

    The CORRECT answer is:

    A. I, II, III   B. I, IV
    C. II, IV   D. III, IV, V
    E. IV, V

12. Philosophers who were *elitist* were
    I. Socrates
    II. Nietzsche
    III. John Stuart Mill
    IV. Kant
    V. Aristotle
    The CORRECT answer is:

    A. I *only*
    B. I, II
    C. I, II, III, IV
    D. I, II, V
    E. IV, V

13. In philosophy of law, *conventionalism* means
    I. a person is immoral only if he/she breaks the law
    II. a person does wrong only if there is a law against it
    III. laws are based on nothing more than social convention
    IV. laws are based on moral principles of society
    V. none of the above
    The CORRECT answer is:

    A. I, III
    B. II, III
    C. II, IV
    D. IV *only*
    E. V *only*

14. EROS AND CIVILIZATION was written by

    A. B. F. Skinner
    B. Thoreau
    C. Freud
    D. Russell
    E. none of the above

15. The theory of dualism generates the philosophical problems of
    I. nominalism
    II. epiphenomenalism
    III. identity theory
    IV. reductionism
    V. none of the above
    The CORRECT answer is:

    A. I, II, III
    B. II, III
    C. II, III, IV
    D. III, IV
    E. V *only*

16. According to common sense realism,
    I. people who doubt whether they exist are crazy
    II. Cartesian doubt is absurd
    III. objects are real whether we see them or not
    IV. when we think we perceive something, and we have evidence, it is there
    V. all of the above
    The CORRECT answer is:

    A. I, II, III, IV
    B. II, III, IV
    C. II, IV
    D. III, IV
    E. V *only*

17. "The world exhibits order, therefore it was produced by an intelligent designer." This argument is called the

    A. ontological argument
    B. cosmological argument
    C. teleological argument
    D. argument from faith
    E. none of the above

18. The theological view that God inheres in all living creatures is
    I. polytheism
    II. monotheism
    III. animism
    IV. pantheism
    V. all of the above
The CORRECT answer is:

    A. I only
    B. II only
    C. II, III
    D. III, IV
    E. V only

19. Rule-utilitarianism claims that

    A. individual actions do not need to be morally evaluated
    B. the principle of utility is the proper criterion of right conduct
    C. act-utilitarianism is too time-consuming
    D. probabilities support moral rules
    E. all of the above

20. Act-utilitarianism claims that

    A. some actions are exceptions to moral rules
    B. the principle of utility is the proper criterion of right conduct
    C. rule-utilitarianism leads to bad consequences
    D. only acts which maximize future happiness ought to be done
    E. all of the above

21. THE PHILOSOPHY OF RIGHT was written by

    A. Marx
    B. Hegel
    C. Schiller
    D. Kant
    E. Pascal

22. Platonism holds that
    I. our senses give us reliable knowledge about the world
    II. there is a hidden, universal and unchanging world behind what we see
    III. all truth is universal
    IV. individuals are not significant overall
    V. all of the above
The CORRECT answer is:

    A. I, II
    B. II, III
    C. II, III, IV
    D. II, IV
    E. V only

23. Philosophy of education concerns

    A. elucidation of proper didactics
    B. pedagogy
    C. propaganda
    D. political justification
    E. none of the above

24. Philosophy *primarily* deals with statements that are

    I. particulars
    II. generalizations
    III. universalizations
    IV. none of the above
    V. all of the above

    The CORRECT answer is:

    A. I, III   B. II *only*
    C. II, III   D. IV *only*
    E. V *only*

25. Some *fundamental* questions dealt with by MOST philosophers are

    I. space
    II. time
    III. ideas
    IV. death
    V. all of the above

    The CORRECT answer is:

    A. I, II, III   B. I, III, IV
    C. II, III   D. III, IV
    E. V *only*

26. The proposition that the square of the hypotenuse equals the sum of the squares on the other two sides was discovered by

    A. Descartes   B. Pythagoras
    C. Leibniz   D. Aristotle
    E. none of the above

27. Atomists believe that

    A. the world is made up of combinations of the smallest particles
    B. nuclear physics is the way of the future
    C. the world is made up of water
    D. earth, wind, fire and water make up reality
    E. none of the above

28. Zeno's paradox tries to prove that

    I. no one can get something from nothing
    II. nothing can go through space because first it must go through half the distance, and half of that distance, etc.
    III. space is infinitely divisible
    IV. time is subjective
    V. none of the above

    The CORRECT answer is:

A. I, II	B. II only
C. II, III	D. III, IV
E. V only	

29. A *deductive* argument which leads to a contradiction   29._____
    I. shows that the premise is false
    II. is the best kind of logic
    III. characterizes the *reductio ad absurdum*
    IV. is the standard type of syllogism
    V. none of the above
    The CORRECT answer is:

A. I, III	B. II, III
C. II, III, IV	D. IV only
E. V only	

30. The psychologist who was NOT a physical determinist is   30._____

A. Skinner	B. Pavlov
C. Watson	D. Freud
E. none of the above	

31. The philosopher who did NOT believe the soul is made up of distinct parts is   31._____

A. Plato	B. Socrates
C. Aristotle	D. Descartes
E. Hume	

32. Platonism is characterized by   32._____
    I. materialism
    II. pantheism
    III. empiricism
    IV. idealism
    V. universals
    The CORRECT answer is:

A. I only	B. II only
C. II, III	D. III, IV, V
E. IV, V	

33. Parmenides, with Socrates, argued the point that   33._____

    A. life begins at death
    B. existence is necessary
    C. nothing cannot be something
    D. everything is nothing
    E. none of the above

34. In THE REPUBLIC, women are   34._____
    I. treated as slaves
    II. free to have children by any man
    III. confined to childcare activities
    IV. capable of being philosopher-kings
    V. the equals of men
    The CORRECT answer is:

A. I, II, IV B. II, III, IV
C. II, IV D. II, IV, V
E. IV, V

35. The ancient city-state whose politics inspired Plato's vision in THE REPUBLIC was

   A. Athens B. Selinus
   C. Crete D. Corinth
   E. Sparta

36. An argument that can be repeated over and over, without reaching an end, is

   A. a favorite of ancient philosophers
   B. an infinite regress
   C. a reductio ad absurdum
   D. modus tollens
   E. none of the above

37. The "Symposium," in which Socrates argues that true love requires wisdom in AT LEAST one of the lovers, is a(n)

   A. Platonic dialogue
   B. account of a class at the Academy
   C. argument between Aristotle and Socrates
   D. drinking party
   E. all of the above

38. One of Socrates' famous claims was that

   A. only my own consciousness can be proved
   B. life begins at death
   C. life is meaningless
   D. wisdom is realizing one is ignorant
   E. none of the above

39. A philosophical tract that is NOT written by Plato is

   A. ORGANON B. PHAEDO
   C. SYMPOSIUM D. MENO
   E. REPUBLIC

40. One of the occupations NOT found in THE REPUBLIC is

   A. guardian B. worker
   C. soldier D. philosopher
   E. musician

41. According to Socrates, the soul alternates between life in and out of a body. Therefore,
   I. it is irrelevant what we learn in school
   II. learning is remembering
   III. death is no great tragedy
   IV. man is immortal
   V. none of the above
   The CORRECT answer is:

A. I, III
B. II, III
C. II, III, IV
D. II, IV
E. V only

42. Given the argument offered by Socrates in the CRITO that each citizen is morally obligated to obey the law, Socrates would have to
    I. agree with Martin Luther King that it is morally right to disobey unjust laws, like those prohibiting blacks to sit in the front of the bus
    II. disagree with Martin Luther King, and say that King is morally obligated to sit in the back of the bus
    III. disagree with King and suggest that if he does not like the laws in this country, he can leave
    IV. agree with King that unjust laws have no right to be enforced
    V. obey every law legitimately passed, even if it killed him
    The CORRECT answer is:

    A. I only
    B. I, IV
    C. II, III
    D. II, III, V
    E. III, V

43. The philosopher referred to as "The Stagyrite," and "The Philosopher" is

    A. Socrates
    B. Plato
    C. Aristotle
    D. Parmenides
    E. Pythagoras

44. Aristotle studied under

    A. Socrates
    B. Plato
    C. Parmenides
    D. Pythagoras
    E. Aeschylus

45. Aristotle's theories about _____ have been disproved.
    I. ethics
    II. politics
    III. biology
    IV. logic
    V. physics
    The CORRECT answer is:

    A. I, II
    B. I, III
    C. II, III
    D. III, IV, V
    E. III, V

46. A *primary* component of Aristotle's logic is

    A. matter
    B. form
    C. structure
    D. syllogism
    E. all of the above

47. "All men are mortal. Socrates is a man. Therefore, Socrates is mortal."
    This argument is
    I. invalid
    II. unsound
    III. syllogistic
    IV. valid
    V. sound
    The CORRECT answer is:

    A. I, II
    B. II only
    C. III, IV
    D. III, IV, V
    E. IV, V

48. Aristotle's logic is called
    I. prepositional calculus
    II. Pythagorean mathematics
    III. theory of categories
    IV. theory of forms
    V. syllogistic
    The CORRECT answer is:

    A. I only
    B. I, III
    C. III, V
    D. IV, V
    E. V only

49. Philosophical schools advocating a withdrawal from public life are
    I. Cartesian rationalism
    II. Socratic idealism
    III. stoicism
    IV. cynicism
    V. utilitarianism
    The CORRECT answer is:

    A. I only
    B. II only
    C. II, III
    D. III, IV
    E. III, IV, V

50. Virtue, for Aristotle, was
    I. the mean between the extremes
    II. zeal over righteousness
    III. impossible to attain
    IV. incompatible with wealth and position
    V. compatible with wealth and position
    The CORRECT answer is:

    A. I, V
    B. II, III
    C. II, IV
    D. II, III, V
    E. V only

KEY (CORRECT ANSWERS)

1. D	11. E	21. B	31. D	41. C
2. A	12. D	22. C	32. E	42. D
3. D	13. B	23. B	33. C	43. C
4. C	14. C	24. C	34. D	44. B
5. C	15. C	25. E	35. E	45. E
6. D	16. B	26. B	36. B	46. B
7. D	17. C	27. A	37. D	47. D
8. D	18. D	28. C	38. D	48. C
9. E	19. E	29. A	39. A	49. D
10. C	20. E	30. D	40. E	50. A

EXAMINATION SECTION
TEST 1

DIRECTIONS: Each question or incomplete statement is followed by several suggested answers or completions. Select the one that BEST answers the question or completes the statement. *PRINT THE LETTER OF THE CORRECT ANSWER IN THE SPACE AT THE RIGHT.*

1. Aristotle's theories are characterized *primarily* by their

   A. emphasis upon universal truths
   B. scientific accuracy
   C. emphasis upon teleology
   D. brevity
   E. all of the above

   1.____

2. Euclid's geometry is characterized by
   I. inductive generalizations
   II. enumerative induction
   III. deduction
   IV. axiomatic precision
   V. all of the above
   The CORRECT answer is:

   A. I, II
   B. II, III
   C. III only
   D. III, IV
   E. V only

   2.____

3. A Roman philosopher who taught Nero was

   A. Epictetus
   B. Chrysippus
   C. Zeno
   D. Marcus Aurelius
   E. Seneca

   3.____

4. In his "Meditations," Marcus Aurelius advocates
   I. a withdrawal from life following stoicism
   II. an involvement in life as in Aristotle
   III. using power politics to achieve goals
   IV. using persuasion and argument to achieve goals
   V. separating private and public life
   The CORRECT answer is:

   A. I only
   B. II, IV
   C. III, IV
   D. III, IV, V
   E. IV, V

   4.____

5. The philosopher who wrote the CONFESSIONS, in which he listed his many sins, and who later became a saint, is

   A. Descartes
   B. Aquinas
   C. Anselm
   D. Constantine
   E. Augustine

   5.____

6. Medieval scholasticism is *closely* associated with the Greek philosopher   6._____

   A. Plato   B. Aristotle
   C. Socrates   D. Pythagoras
   E. Zeo

7. Thomism, in Catholic theology, originates with the philosopher   7._____

   A. Plato   B. Anselm
   C. Aquinas   D. Augustine
   E. none of the above

8. The *law of double effect* in Thomistic theology was designed to   8._____

   A. excuse an immoral action that is a necessary accompaniment of a good action
   B. show that only Catholics can be moral
   C. show the complexity of God's ways
   D. reveal the importance of consequences in moral thinking
   E. show that we can do two things at once

9. One of Aquinas' MAJOR philosophical accomplishments was   9._____

   A. showing the mystery of God
   B. resurrecting Platonic idealism in theology
   C. inventing mathematical systems
   D. proving that God created humans with free will
   E. proving that God has preordinated what humans will do

10. The philosopher who is still the *official* founder of Catholic theology is   10._____

    A. St. Augustine   B. St. Aquinas
    C. St. Anselm   D. Duns Scotus
    E. none of the above

11. Until St. Thomas Aquinas, Catholic theology disparaged   11._____

    A. faith   B. revelation
    C. reason   D. mystery
    E. women

12. Duns Scotus, disagreeing with Plato, said that   12._____

    A. will rules reason
    B. reason rules will
    C. logic rules thinking
    D. faith rules logic
    E. knowledge is based on universals

13. "Occam's Razor," proposed by William of Occam, is the view that   13._____

    A. whatever people believe is true
    B. truth is personal and not logical
    C. knowledge is based on experience
    D. simple explanations are always preferred
    E. complexity is the normal way of the world

14. Machiavelli wrote

    A. THE MEDITATIONS
    B. THE CONFESSIONS
    C. THE PRINCE
    D. THE REPUBLIC
    E. THE LEVIATHAN

15. One of the MOST important concepts in Machiavelli's political philosophy is

    A. prudence
    B. morality
    C. religion
    D. the papacy
    E. aristocracy

16. Two thinkers very much responsible for theological revolution in the period of the Enlightenment are _____ and _____.

    A. Descartes, Spinoza
    B. Leibniz, Descartes
    C. Luther, Calvin
    D. Calvin, Maimonides
    E. Erasmus, Maimonides

17. Copernicus was a philosopher who
    I. angered the Catholics and Lutherans both with his theory
    II. angered the Catholics but was praised by the Lutherans for his theory
    III. created a heliocentric hypothesis
    IV. challenged the omnipotence of God
    V. all of the above

    The CORRECT answer is:

    A. I only
    B. I, III
    C. II, III
    D. IV only
    E. V only

18. Philosophers who greatly hastened scientific knowledge are
    I. Newton
    II. Kepler
    III. Copernicus
    IV. Galileo
    V. all of the above

    The CORRECT answer is:

    A. I, II, III
    B. I, III, IV
    C. II, IV
    D. III, IV
    E. V only

19. The revolutionary idea advocated by Galileo, Copernicus, and Kepler was that the
    I. earth is not the center of the universe
    II. earth is the center of the universe
    III. planets orbit around the sun
    IV. sun is in orbit around the earth
    V. none of the above

    The CORRECT answer is:

    A. I only
    B. I, III
    C. II only
    D. II, IV
    E. V only

20. Galileo became famous for a scientific hypothesis
    I. concerning motions of bodies
    II. concerning static relationships of objects
    III. improving the theory of dynamics
    IV. proving that knowledge is impossible
    V. all of the above
    The CORRECT answer is:

    A. I, III
    B. I, III, IV
    C. II, III
    D. II, III, IV
    E. V only

21. A philosopher who profoundly influenced Thomas Hobbes' political philosophy is

    A. Galileo
    B. Aristotle
    C. Plato
    D. Augustine
    E. Descartes

22. In 1640, Hobbes left England for France because of the publication of his book

    A. THE CONFESSIONS
    B. THE LEVIATHAN
    C. THE PRINCE
    D. THE REPUBLIC
    E. THE MEDITATIONS

23. The *primary* focus of Hobbes' political theory was

    A. sovereignty
    B. peace
    C. war
    D. power
    E. morality

24. For Hobbes, the WORST possible thing for a country is

    A. civil society
    B. the state of nature
    C. corruption
    D. civil war
    E. foreign war

25. The view that the mental and the physical are separate is called

    A. epiphenomenalism
    B. empiricism
    C. idealism
    D. dualism
    E. materialism

26. Spinoza wrote
    I. THE ETHICS
    II. THE LEVIATHAN
    III. THE REPUBLIC
    IV. THE TRACTATUS THEOLOGICO-POLITICUS
    V. none of the above
    The CORRECT answer is:

    A. I only
    B. I, IV
    C. II, IV
    D. III, IV
    E. V only

27. Democracy was defended by

   A. Plato
   B. Aristotle
   C. Machiavelli
   D. Hobbes
   E. Spinoza

28. THE MONADOLOGY was written by

   A. Maimonides
   B. Spinoza
   C. Descartes
   D. Leibniz
   E. Hobbes

29. The country responsible for promoting empiricist philosophy the MOST was

   A. ancient Greece
   B. ancient Rome
   C. France
   D. Germany
   E. Britain

30. The *primary* British empiricists were

   A. Hobbes, Hume, Bacon
   B. Locke, Berkeley, Hume
   C. Locke, Leibniz, Spinoza
   D. Spinoza, Hobbes, Kant
   E. Bacon, Newton, Kepler

31. Empiricism holds that the mind is *originally*
   I. full of innate mechanisms
   II. comprised of innate ideas
   III. devoid of innate ideas
   IV. a blank sheet
   V. none of the above

   The CORRECT answer is:

   A. I, II
   B. I, III
   C. III, IV
   D. IV *only*
   E. V *only*

32. According to British empiricists, human thoughts are
   I. copied from sense experience
   II. vague shadows of physical objects
   III. clearer and more reliable than empirical data
   IV. dependent upon logical validity
   V. worthless

   The CORRECT answer is:

   A. I, II
   B. I, III
   C. II, III, IV
   D. III, IV, V
   E. V *only*

33. Doctrines of particular political importance gained from John Locke were
    I. private property
    II. divine right of kings
    III. natural rights
    IV. positive law
    V. none of the above
    The CORRECT answer is:

    A. I, II, III
    B. I, III
    C. III
    D. II, IV
    E. V only

34. The phrase *"Life, liberty and the pursuit of happiness"*
    I. was stolen from Hobbes' LEVIATHAN
    II. is derived from Locke's philosophy
    III. was changed from its original form, "Life, liberty, and the protection of property"
    IV. represents natural rights in liberal political theory
    V. all of the above
    The CORRECT answer is:

    A. I, II, III
    B. I, III, IV
    C. II, III, IV
    D. II, IV
    E. V only

35. The British empiricist philosophy LEAST compatible with common sense is that of

    A. Locke
    B. Hume
    C. Berkeley
    D. Hobbes
    E. Bacon

36. The phrase that BEST describes Berkeley's epistemology is

    A. British empiricism
    B. logical positivism
    C. existentialism
    D. materialism
    E. subjective idealism

37. Hume proved that we have NO evidence for believing in
    I. cause and effect
    II. human knowledge
    III. love
    IV. wisdom
    V. all of the above
    The CORRECT answer is:

    A. I, II
    B. I, II, III
    C. II only
    D. II, III, IV
    E. V only

38. THE CONFESSIONS, THE SOCIAL CONTRACT and EMILE were *all* written by the philosopher

    A. Descartes
    B. Hobbes
    C. Hume
    D. Rousseau
    E. Augustine

39. Kant's metaphysical system emphasized the distinctions between
    I. noumena and phenomena
    II. appearance and reality
    III. love and hate
    IV. reason and passion
    V. things in themselves and things as they appear to us
    The CORRECT answer is:

    A. I, II, III
    B. I, II, V
    C. I, II, IV
    D. II, V
    E. IV, V

40. The MOST fundamental concept(s) in Kant's ethical system is(are)

    A. benevolence
    B. overall happiness
    C. categorical imperative
    D. consequences of our actions
    E. all of the above

41. "Don't vote for Mr. Smith in the upcoming election; he once failed an exam in high school, so he'd probably be unscrupulous."
    The fallacy in this argument is that of

    A. provincialism
    B. questionable cause
    C. questionable classification
    D. ad hominem
    E. slippery slope

42. "The universe, like a watch, must have a maker."
    The fallacy in this argument is that of

    A. provincialism
    B. questionable cause
    C. questionable classification
    D. questionable analogy
    E. slippery slope

43. "Her hair is so long and pretty; I'll bet she has thousands of dates."
    The fallacy in this comment is

    A. provincialism
    B. ad hominem
    C. exaggeration
    D. slippery slope
    E. questionable analogy

44. "Abortion is wrong because it is murder."
    The fallacy in this statement is

    A. provincialism
    B. questionable analogy
    C. questionable classification
    D. begging the question
    E. slippery slope

45. "Either those teachers care for the kids, and avoid a strike, or they strike and show they don't care for the kids." The fallacy in this argument is

    A. provincialism
    B. questionable analogy
    C. false dilemma
    D. straw man
    E. inconsistency

46. "Residents of Cleveland really don't want Mr. Smith for mayor; I asked 17 people in my neighborhood, and they think he shouldn't even run for office."
    The fallacy in this claim is

    A. traditional wisdom
    B. popularity
    C. small sample
    D. questionable classification
    E. ambiguity

47. "The General Surgeon has determined that breathing is dangerous to your health. This conclusion was drawn from a survey of 100 Canadian rats that have died within the past 5 years. All were habitual breathers."
    The fallacy in this argument is

    A. traditional wisdom
    B. popularity
    C. questionable classification
    D. questionable cause
    E. questionable analogy

48. "Of all the married women in the world, 73% wish they had married someone else."
    The fallacy in this claim is that of

    A. suppressed evidence
    B. faulty comparison
    C. ambiguity
    D. unknowable statistic
    E. hasty conclusion

49. "Freedom is wonderful, even if it makes some people feel imprisoned."
    The fallacy in this claim is that of

    A. suppressed evidence
    B. ambiguity
    C. faulty comparison
    D. unknowable statistics
    E. hasty conclusion

50. "Of course we ought to go there; Mr. Jones says so."
    The fallacy here is

    A. suppressed evidence
    B. fallacy of authority
    C. unknowable statistics
    D. hasty conclusion
    E. traditional wisdom

KEY (CORRECT ANSWERS)

1. C	11. C	21. E	31. C	41. D
2. D	12. A	22. B	32. A	42. D
3. E	13. D	23. A	33. B	43. B
4. B	14. C	24. D	34. C	44. D
5. E	15. A	25. D	35. C	45. C
6. B	16. C	26. B	36. E	46. C
7. E	17. B	27. D	37. A	47. D
8. A	18. E	28. D	38. D	48. D
9. D	19. B	29. E	39. B	49. A
10. B	20. A	30. B	40. C	50. B

TEST 2

DIRECTIONS: Each question or incomplete statement is followed by several suggested answers or completions. Select the one that BEST answers the question or completes the statement. *PRINT THE LETTER OF THE CORRECT ANSWER IN THE SPACE AT THE RIGHT.*

1. One of G. E. Moore's MAIN claims as a common sense realist is that
    I. reality is actually much as it appears to us
    II. the fact that physics describes reality differently from our ordinary way of doing so, shows we are wrong
    III. theories that prove that what we see is not real are false
    IV. philosophical analysis can get carried away with itself
    V. all of the above
   The CORRECT answer is:

   A. I, II, III
   C. II, III
   E. V only
   B. I, III, IV
   D. II, III, IV

2. Ordinary language analysis is *fundamentally* a

   A. fallacious technique used by logicians
   B. method used by 17th century French thinkers
   C. 20th century philosophical method
   D. topic studied by linguists
   E. all of the above

3. "Theories showing that I do not know I am holding this pencil in my hand right now must be false because they conclude this."
   This argument, made by Moore, is
    I. a cheap argument to avoid the real issue
    II. question-begging
    III. a version of reductio ad absurdum
    IV. clever
    V. all of the above
   The CORRECT answer is:

   A. I only
   C. II, III, IV
   E. V only
   B. I, II
   D. III, IV

4. The theory of sense-data was a natural by-product of

   A. rationalism
   C. empiricism
   E. realism
   B. materialism
   D. nominalism

5. The chief problem with epistemological skepticism is that

   A. if it is true, no one knows anything
   B. if it is false, many philosophers have worked for nothing
   C. it is argued sloppily
   D. it is difficult to refute
   E. all of the above

6. One thing *challenged* by Humean skepticism is

    A. deriving a conclusion from enumerative induction
    B. our own existence
    C. God
    D. math
    E. none of the above

7. One *fundamental* concept in phenomenology is

    A. love
    B. death
    C. knowledge
    D. structuralism
    E. intentionality

8. Anarchism is a political philosophy espoused by _____ and _____.

    A. Karl Marx, Rousseau
    B. Thomas Hobbes, Locke
    C. Bakunin, Thoreau
    D. Stirner, Proudhon
    E. Emerson, Jefferson

9. Albert Camus was the author of
    I. BEING AND NOTHINGNESS
    II. THE MYTH OF SISYPHUS
    III. THE STRANGER
    IV. THE PLAGUE
    V. THE CRITIQUE OF DIALECTICAL REASON

    The CORRECT answer is:

    A. I, II
    B. II, III, IV
    C. III, IV
    D. III, V
    E. IV *only*

10. Jean-Paul Sartre was the author of
    I. BEING AND NOTHINGNESS
    II. THE MYTH OF SISYPHUS
    III. THE STRANGER
    IV. THE PLAGUE
    V. THE CRITIQUE OF DIALECTICAL REASON

    The CORRECT answer is:

    A. I *only*
    B. I, II
    C. I, IV, V
    D. I, V
    E. V *only*

11. Existentialism gets its name from its claims that

    A. no one exists
    B. solipsism is silly
    C. emotions can prove things as well as reason
    D. humans are helpless victims of human life
    E. we do not choose to exist

12. Some typical claims made by existentialists are that
    I. life is absurd
    II. man's reason will save him from sin
    III. God is a necessary component of human life
    IV. truth is not universal but individual
    V. all of the above
    The CORRECT answer is:

    A. I only
    B. I, IV
    C. II, IV
    D. II, III, IV
    E. V only

13. The theory existentialism challenged MOST was

    A. nominalism
    B. empiricism
    C. rationalism
    D. idealism
    E. materialism

14. Heidegger wrote the phenomenological and existential opus

    A. BEING AND NOTHINGNESS
    B. CRITIQUE OF DIALECTICAL REASON
    C. CRITIQUE OF PURE REASON
    D. BEING AND TIME
    E. none of the above

15. Some MAJOR philosophers in the field of aesthetics are _____ and _____.
    I. Croce, Coleridge
    II. Dewey, Pater
    III. Schiller, Tolstoy
    IV. Hume, Kant
    V. Descartes, Leibniz
    The CORRECT answer is:

    A. I, II, III
    B. II, III, IV
    C. III, IV
    D. IV, V
    E. V only

16. The existentialist philosopher famous for claiming that *"God is dead"* is

    A. Sartre
    B. Kierkegaard
    C. Nietzsche
    D. Heidegger
    E. Camus

17. The existentialist philosopher used and distorted by Hitler was

    A. Sartre
    B. Kierkegaard
    C. Nietzsche
    D. Heidegger
    E. Camus

18. The concept of the *ubermensch* was part of the existentialist philosophy of

    A. Sartre
    B. Kierkegaard
    C. Nietzsche
    D. Heidegger
    E. Camus

19. Standard themes of existentialist writers are
    I. love
    II. death
    III. sickness
    IV. meaning
    V. angst
    The CORRECT answer is:

    A. I, II
    B. II, III
    C. II, III, V
    D. III, IV, V
    E. all of the above

20. Correspondence theory states that

    A. if you do not know how theories interrelate, you cannot achieve knowledge
    B. statements that are logically valid correspond to rules of truth
    C. statements that correspond to objective reality are true
    D. reality corresponds with our minds
    E. all of the above

21. The *primary* problem with correspondence theory is that

    A. it assumes a metaphysics in order to judge the truth of statements
    B. hardly any philosophers have argued for it
    C. it is too simple and neat to be valid
    D. no one really uses it
    E. all of the above

22. Some of the MAJOR dilemmas posed by epistemology and metaphysics are that
    I. both require at least a high school education to discuss
    II. neither has achieved consensus in the philosophical community
    III. we probably don't know anything *except* that we don't know anything
    IV. each one presupposes the other
    V. all of the above
    The CORRECT answer is:

    A. I, II
    B. II, III
    C. II, IV
    D. III, IV
    E. V *only*

23. Problems with the cosmological argument for the existence of God include that
    I. it applies only to believers
    II. it is patently false
    III. there is so much evidence that it takes too much time to prove
    IV. the evidence is not conclusive
    V. there is evidence to the contrary
    The CORRECT answer is:

    A. I, II, III
    B. II, III
    C. II, IV
    D. III, IV
    E. IV, V

24. The interesting thing about first-person reports is that

    A. they are not challenged by third-person reports
    B. they claim epistemological priority
    C. they cannot be proven false
    D. to claim them is to verify them
    E. all of the above

25. The *primary* method that is used to prove the existence of others is

    A. empirical evidence
    B. common knowledge
    C. circumstantial evidence
    D. argument by analogy
    E. our intimacy with our mothers

26. Color is philosophically interesting because

    A. it proves that some knowledge is gained empirically
    B. we do not know if others see the same colors we do
    C. objects do not have color
    D. it is subjective
    E. all of the above

27. Moore's common sense philosophy was really
    I. a cop-out from the difficulties of metaphysics
    II. a form of common sense realism
    III. similar to some philosophers from Scotland
    IV. compatible with the theories of Thomas Reid
    V. an epistemological view

    The CORRECT answer is:

    A. I, II, III   B. I, II, III, IV
    C. II, III, IV, V   D. III, IV, V
    E. all of the above

28. The philosopher famous for having distinguished *knowledge by acquaintance* from *knowledge by description* is

    A. Hume   B. Russell
    C. Moore   D. Ayer
    E. Hamlyn

29. Reductionism in 20th century philosophy is *usually* associated with
    I. physicalism
    II. determinism
    III. idealism
    IV. aesthetics
    V. psychology

    The CORRECT answer is:

    A. I, II, V   B. II, III, V
    C. II, IV   D. III, IV, V
    E. all of the above

30. Logical atomism was a theory *primarily* promoted by

    A. Moore
    B. Russell
    C. Ayer
    D. Schlick
    E. Hamlyn

31. The *fundamental* claim of LOGICAL ATOMISM is that

    A. physics is mistaken
    B. only quantum mechanics comes close to the truth
    C. sense data are atomic particulars
    D. the ultimate constituents of reality are atomic particulars
    E. none of the above

32. Universities *usually* associated with ordinary language analysis are
    I. Harvard
    II. Princeton
    III. Notre Dame
    IV. Oxford
    V. Cambridge

    The CORRECT answer is:

    A. I, II
    B. II, III
    C. III, IV, V
    D. III, V
    E. IV, V

33. An analytic truth
    I. is tautological
    II. cannot be false
    III. is quite probably true
    IV. is unknowable by humans
    V. is true by definition

    The CORRECT answer is:

    A. I, II
    B. I, II, III
    C. II *only*
    D. II, IV, V
    E. II, V

34. An *a priori* truth
    I. is tautological
    II. cannot be false
    III. is quite probably true
    IV. is unknowable by humans
    V. is true by definition

    The CORRECT answer is:

    A. I, II, IV, V
    B. I, V
    C. II, V
    D. III, IV, V
    E. IV, V

35. Some statements are

    A. true analytically and a priori
    B. true analytically but not a priori
    C. false analytically

D. false a priori
E. all of the above

36. The difference between (a) "All effects are caused," and (b) "All events are caused" is that

   A. (a) is true but (b) is false
   B. (b) is false but (a) is true
   C. (a) is analytic whereas (b) is a priori
   D. (b) is analytic whereas (a) is a priori
   E. (a) is analytic whereas (b) is synthetic and a priori

37. The 20th century philosopher who was NOT part of the ordinary language school of philosophy is

   A. Ryle   B. Austin
   C. Strawson   D. Dewey
   E. Russell

38. The 20th century philosophical school of ordinary language analysis is *chiefly* characterized by its belief that

   A. philosophers use too much jargon
   B. the best language is the simplest
   C. philosophical problems can be solved by analyzing language
   D. the way we use words reveals philosophical assumptions
   E. only English-speaking philosophers are legitimate

39. The skeptical claim, *"No one has any knowledge,"* is

   A. false   B. true
   C. paradoxical   D. fallaciously inferred
   E. depressing

40. Some MAJOR problems of concern to 20th century Anglo-American philosophers are

   A. love and death   B. being and nothingness
   C. values   D. existence of other minds
   E. none of the above

41. A synthetic statement

   A. is also analytic
   B. is also a priori
   C. can be proved by definition
   D. cannot be false
   E. provides information

42. The philosophers who are transcendentalists in metaphysics are
   I. Moore   II. Kant   III. Russell   IV. Hume   V. Locke

   The CORRECT answer is:

   A. I, II, III   B. II, III
   C. II, III, IV   D. II, III, IV, V
   E. III, IV, V

43. Philosophers who believe in transcendental metaphysics believe that ultimate reality

    A. can be known *only* by God
    B. is revealed through sensory experience
    C. cannot be known without logic
    D. is no different from ordinary perception
    E. all of the above

44. One of the famous views propagated by Ludwig Wittgenstein is

    A. common sense realism
    B. that the best proof is to show necessary and sufficient conditions
    C. that quantifying propositions increases philosophical knowledge by increasing precision
    D. that it is impossible to define most words in our vocabularies
    E. that there is a universal structure to language

45. Strawson, in discussing the existence of other persons, claims that

    A. there is no evidence for the existence of others
    B. there is only very shaky evidence for the existence of others
    C. the concept of a person proves the existence of others
    D. only persons worry about whether there are others
    E. all of the above

46. The 20th century philosopher who emphasized Descartes' claim that *"I am not in my body like a pilot in a shop"* is

    A. Russell   B. Strawson
    C. Ryle   D. Moore
    E. Wittgenstein

47. Problems with Cartesianism in epistemology are that
    I. when we are unconscious we do not exist
    II. it is at variance with our senses
    III. it logically leads to solipsism
    IV. it logically leads to skepticism
    V. it confuses modern philosophers

    The CORRECT answer is:

    A. I, II, III, IV   B. I, III, IV
    C. II, III, IV   D. III, IV, V
    E. IV, V

48. Strawson claimed that

    A. only love can break a heart
    B. persons are self-ascribers of P-predicates
    C. tautologies are not admissible as evidence of our existence
    D. empiricism should be strictly applied in philosophical analysis
    E. all of the above

49. Wittgenstein argued that private languages are
    I. difficult to learn
    II. impossible to imagine
    III. conceptually confused
    IV. out of fashion
    V. useful for personal meditation
   The CORRECT answer is:

   A. I, II, III
   B. II only
   C. II, III
   D. II, III, IV, V
   E. III, V

50. The BEST evidence to use in discussing meaning, according to Wittgenstein, is
    I. the dictionary
    II. other people's opinions
    III. how we behave when doing it
    IV. how we refer to it in discussion
    V. how we would teach it to others
   The CORRECT answer is:

   A. I only
   B. II, III
   C. II, IV, V
   D. III, IV, V
   E. IV, V

KEY (CORRECT ANSWERS)

1. B	11. E	21. A	31. D	41. E
2. C	12. B	22. C	32. E	42. B
3. D	13. C	23. E	33. A	43. C
4. C	14. D	24. E	34. B	44. D
5. D	15. A	25. D	35. E	45. C
6. A	16. C	26. E	36. E	46. B
7. E	17. C	27. C	37. D	47. A
8. C	18. C	28. B	38. C	48. B
9. B	19. E	29. A	39. C	49. C
10. D	20. C	30. B	40. D	50. D

EXAMINATION SECTION
TEST 1

DIRECTIONS: Each question or incomplete statement is followed by several suggested answers or completions. Select the one that BEST answers the question or completes the statement. *PRINT THE LETTER OF THE CORRECT ANSWER IN THE SPACE AT THE RIGHT.*

1. The philosopher who claimed that *"I never can catch myself at any time without a perception"* is

   A. Hume
   B. Kant
   C. Russell
   D. Nietzsche
   E. Ryle

   1._____

2. A *frequently* used concept in discussions of private languages is

   A. love
   B. fear
   C. worry
   D. doubt
   E. pain

   2._____

3. One reason to DENY the existence of private languages is that

   A. doing so makes it easier to refute skepticism
   B. the existence of others is easier to prove without them
   C. it presupposes strict empiricism
   D. it creates more problems than it solves
   E. all of the above

   3._____

4. Russell's opinion of ordinary language analysis was that
   I. it helped clear up common philosophical confusions
   II. it misleads philosophers into believing what they see
   III. metaphysical assumptions are built into language
   IV. only science can reveal reality, not language
   V. all of the above
   The CORRECT answer is:

   A. I, II, IV
   B. II, III, IV
   C. II, IV
   D. III, IV
   E. V *only*

   4._____

5. The MOST notable advocate of logical atomism is

   A. Ayer
   B. Strawson
   C. Russell
   D. Moore
   E. Wittgenstein

   5._____

6. Neutral monism claims that

   A. matter is neither good nor bad
   B. only one philosophical system can be true
   C. ethics is illegitimate
   D. there is only one form of matter, whether physical or mental
   E. none of the above

   6._____

125

7. Logical positivism is a 20th century philosophy famous for

   A. challenging views on the basis of their falsity
   B. challenging views on the basis of their meaninglessness
   C. challenging views on the basis of their antiquity
   D. not challenging any views
   E. challenging views just to challenge

8. An everyday fact that proves transcendental metaphysics and argues *against* empiricism is that
   I. sticks in glasses of water are not really bent
   II. we frequently think we are awake when we are asleep
   III. only educated philosophers can do enough logic to prove metaphysics
   IV. ordinary people do not care about ultimate reality
   V. none of the above

   The CORRECT answer is:

   A. I, II
   B. I, II, III
   C. I, III, IV
   D. II, IV
   E. V only

9. A *central* concept in Strawson's metaphysics is

   A. neutral monism
   B. third person statements
   C. basic particulars
   D. logical fictions
   E. none of the above

10. Strawson and Russell DISAGREED, in their metaphysical theories, about whether or not
    I. reality was coherent
    II. reality was unified
    III. reality existed at all
    IV. we could ever know what is real
    V. philosophers earned a living

    The CORRECT answer is:

    A. I, II
    B. I, III
    C. II, IV
    D. II, IV, V
    E. IV, V

11. A *fundamental* criticism of utilitarian ethics is that it

    A. is inarticulately stated by its proponents
    B. is confusing to apply in practice
    C. requires moral agents to be unfair
    D. permits moral agents to be unfair
    E. is too narrow in its application

12. The four-step procedure recommended by utilitarian moral theory is:

    A. (1) plan your act; (2) become aware of your motives; (3) universalize; (4) act
    B. (1) read the Bible; (2) ask your parents; (3) flip a coin; (4) act
    C. (1) consider all alternatives; (2) calculate the consequences; (3) figure out utilities; (4) maximize happiness

D. (1) take a survey of utilities; (2) discount the utilities of anyone not present; (3) maximize the cardinal utilities involved; (4) act
E. (1) consider the moral rules in your theory; (2) decide whether the act involved is covered by a rule; (3) determine which rule; (4) act

13. Problems with the four-step procedure in the previous question are that it
    I. is too time-consuming
    II. is not useful for ignorant people
    III. is too narrow in its application
    IV. makes the same act right and wrong at different times
    V. requires that one can read the future
    The CORRECT answer is:

    A. I, II, III, IV
    B. I, II, IV, V
    C. I, IV
    D. I, IV, V
    E. IV, V

14. Utilitarians defend their procedure by saying that

    A. we use probabilities to predict the future
    B. the best results can be obtained by using it
    C. reason and calculation should be valued over common sense
    D. what is right or wrong is not as obvious as it seems
    E. all of the above

15. Deontology is *primarily* based upon the fact that

    A. everyone already knows the difference between right and wrong
    B. since no one knows what is right or wrong, it does not matter
    C. some actions are wrong by their very nature
    D. why people love calculations cannot be fathomed
    E. prudence is irrelevant to ethics

16. Utilitarianism is a form of
    I. metaphysics
    II. consequentialism
    III. teleological theory
    IV. absolutism
    V. nominalism
    The CORRECT answer is:

    A. I, II, III
    B. II, III
    C. II, III, IV
    D. II, IV, V
    E. III, IV, V

17. Deontology can be characterized as being

    A. in opposition to consequentialism
    B. in opposition to absolutism
    C. relativistic
    D. nominalistic
    E. teleological

18. Things considered *important* by deontological ethics but *unimportant* by utilitarianism are _____ and _____.

    A. life, liberty
    B. love, death
    C. knowledge, education
    D. actions, consequences
    E. motives; intentions

19. The principle of Pareto Optimality in political theory claims that

    A. if a state is optimal for Pareto, it ought to be achieved
    B. optimality can be measured *only* by cardinal utilities
    C. optimality can be measured *only* by ordinary utilities
    D. optimality is achieved if no one can be made better off without making someone else worse off
    E. all of the above

20. One of the *fundamental* problems with Kant's version of deontology is that

    A. he stated it so obliquely and obtusely
    B. it rejects utilitarianism
    C. it is counter-intuitive
    D. it allows for no exceptions
    E. it gives no practical application

21. A version of deontology that is NOT absolutist is given by

    A. Ross
    B. Russell
    C. Moore
    D. Strawson
    E. none of the above

22. A *fundamental* concept in non-absolutist deontology is

    A. prima facie
    B. consequentialism
    C. practicality
    D. knowledge
    E. reason

23. Ethical systems that do NOT rely upon empirical calculation and investigation *usually* emphasize

    A. logic
    B. reason
    C. emotion
    D. intuition
    E. education

24. Decision-theoretic dilemmas assume that
    I. agents are altruistic
    II. agents are egoistic
    III. the choices are finite
    IV. agents are maximizers
    V. rationality is normal
    The CORRECT answer is:

    A. I, II, III, IV
    B. I, III, IV, V
    C. II, III, IV, V
    D. III, IV, V
    E. all of the above

25. John Rawls is famous for having written

    A. ANARCHY, STATE AND UTOPIA
    B. A THEORY OF JUSTICE
    C. PRINCIPIA MATHEMATICA
    D. THOUGHT
    E. REASON AND MORALITY

26. A *fundamental* concern in John Rawls' political philosophy is

    A. rights
    B. logic
    C. distribution of wealth
    D. the law
    E. none of the above

27. The MOST controversial principle introduced by Rawls is

    A. that equality of opportunity is primary
    B. the principle of universalization
    C. the principle of paternalism
    D. the difference principle
    E. none of the above

28. Rawls' recommendation for achieving justice DIFFERS from Pareto Optimality in that
    I. the former recommends that most people must be better off
    II. the latter recommends that most people must be better off
    III. only the former seeks to raise the worst off
    IV. only the latter seeks to lower the best off
    V. only the former seeks justice

    The CORRECT answer is:

    A. I, III
    B. II, III
    C. II, IV
    D. II, IV, V
    E. III, V

29. Robert Nozick's political philosophy claims to be

    A. valid and sound
    B. interesting
    C. inherited from Hume
    D. inherited from Locke
    E. inherited from Hobbes

30. The BEST way to characterize the logical positivist's approach to ethics is
    I. to avoid mentioning it
    II. as emotivism
    III. as non-cognitivist
    IV. scrupulous and conscientious
    V. all of the above

    The CORRECT answer is:

    A. I *only*
    B. II, III
    C. II, III, IV
    D. III, IV
    E. V *only*

31. G. E. Moore *chiefly* analyzed the concept of

    A. truth
    B. beauty
    C. justice
    D. wisdom
    E. goodness

32. Marx's theory of historical materialism is *frequently* said to be deterministic. This, however, CANNOT be, since

    A. Marx would have said so if he had meant it
    B. none of his statements lend themselves to that interpretation
    C. he heavily emphasized the dialectical process
    D. he never formally studied psychology
    E. all of the above

33. One of the MOST important concepts in ancient Greek ethics is

    A. noumena
    B. Logos
    C. anthropos
    D. arete
    E. akrasia

34. A popular theory, concerning the nature of justice, offered by Thrasymachus in the REPUBLIC, claims that
    I. there is no such thing
    II. justice is whatever the rulers say it is
    III. might makes right
    IV. everyone would be unfair if he thought he would be undetected
    V. fair-minded people get exploited

    The CORRECT answer is:

    A. I, II, III
    B. II, III, IV
    C. II, IV, V
    D. II, III, IV, V
    E. III, IV, V

35. The beauty of the ontological argument is that, according to St. Anselm, NOT believing that God really exists
    I. shows you haven't read the Bible
    II. results in a contradiction
    III. shows you don't even know what the word "God" means
    IV. is complex and intricate
    V. all of the above

    The CORRECT answer is:

    A. I, IV
    B. II *only*
    C. II, III
    D. II, III, IV
    E. V *only*

36. When confronted by a counter-example of altruism, the egoist denies the point that sometimes people act other than for self-interest by saying that

    A. the agent is only trying to avoid feeling guilty
    B. the person only wants to get to heaven
    C. the feeling of satisfaction is what the individual wants
    D. getting a good reputation is what is really desired
    E. all of the above

37. A MAJOR problem with egoism is that it

    A. is unfalsifiable
    B. is devoid of information
    C. distorts our ordinary way of speaking about altruism and self-interest

D. seems immoral
E. all of the above

38. Hobbes' *primary* opponent in the debate between altruism and egoism was   38._____

   A. Butler
   B. Hume
   C. Locke
   D. Bentham
   E. Mills

39. Techniques of logical analysis that are *frequently* used are   39._____
   I. algorithms
   II. predicate calculus
   III. Venn diagrams
   IV. truth tables
   V. calculators
   The CORRECT answer is:

   A. I, II, III
   B. II, III, IV
   C. III, IV
   D. III, V
   E. IV, V

40. Descartes, in his MEDITATIONS, proved that he knew for certain that   40._____
   I. his body existed
   II. his mind existed
   III. his body and his mind existed
   IV. he was a thinking thing
   V. all of the above
   The CORRECT answer is:

   A. I, II, IV
   B. II, IV
   C. III only
   D. III, IV
   E. V only

41. A MAJOR difference between Hobbes' State of Nature theory and Locke's is that   41._____
   I. in the former, there is no morality in the state of nature
   II. in the latter, there is morality in the state of nature
   III. Locke assumes altruism while Hobbes doesn't
   IV. benevolence is rejected in the latter
   V. all of the above
   The CORRECT answer is:

   A. I, II
   B. I, II, III
   C. I, III, IV
   D. II, IV
   E. V only

42. John Rawls' version of contract theory adds the feature of   42._____

   A. the difference principle
   B. altruistic agents
   C. the original position
   D. the hedonistic calculus
   E. none of the above

43. Hegel thought that the HIGHEST form of revealed Reason, in history, was

    A. God
    B. the state
    C. philosophy
    D. mathematics
    E. none of the above

44. The philosopher whose dialectic technique Marx "turned on its head" was

    A. Plato
    B. Aristotle
    C. Democritus
    D. Hegel
    E. Kant

45. "If you drink a glass of wine tonight, tomorrow you'll want two glasses. The next day you'll probably want three, and before you know it, you'll be an alcoholic. Therefore, you shouldn't drink that glass of wine now."
    The fallacy in this argument is

    A. the naturalistic fallacy
    B. modus tollens
    C. non sequitur
    D. slippery slope
    E. none of the above

46. "Since he punched me in the face for no reason, I have a right to punch him back."
    The fallacy here is

    A. the naturalistic fallacy
    B. modus tollens
    C. slippery slope
    D. non sequitur
    E. two wrongs don't make a right

47. "I know I shouldn't have stolen the secrets, but everybody else does it."
    The fallacy in this argument is

    A. the naturalistic fallacy
    B. common practice
    C. non sequitur
    D. slippery slope
    E. modus tollens

48. "This may not be the best thing to do, but it has always been done this way so far. Therefore, it ought to be done this way now."
    The fallacy in this argument is that of

    A. slippery slope
    B. non sequitur
    C. traditional wisdom
    D. ambiguity
    E. questionable analogy

49. "This is a good thing to do because people in this area always do it this way."
    The fallacy here is that of

    A. ambiguity
    B. questionable cause
    C. tokenism
    D. provincialism
    E. guilt by association

50. *"Of course our company has equal opportunity; one of our top officers is Miss Jones, a black woman."*
    The fallacy here is that of

    A. ambiguity
    B. questionable cause
    C. tokenism
    D. provincialism
    E. hasty conclusion

    50.____

KEY (CORRECT ANSWERS)

1. A	11. D	21. A	31. E	41. A
2. E	12. C	22. A	32. C	42. C
3. E	13. D	23. D	33. B	43. B
4. B	14. E	24. C	34. D	44. D
5. C	15. C	25. B	35. C	45. D
6. D	16. B	26. C	36. E	46. E
7. B	17. A	27. D	37. E	47. B
8. A	18. E	28. E	38. A	48. C
9. C	19. D	29. D	39. C	49. D
10. A	20. D	30. B	40. B	50. C

TEST 2

DIRECTIONS: Each question or incomplete statement is followed by several suggested answers or completions. Select the one that BEST answers the question or completes the statement. *PRINT THE LETTER OF THE CORRECT ANSWER IN THE SPACE AT THE EIGHT.*

1. Social Darwinism claims that
    I. if you want something badly enough, you'll get it
    II. only the fit survive
    III. in human society, everyone is better off if the inferior ones are extinguished
    IV. everyone always acts in his own self-interest
    V. occasionally, altruism is possible
    The CORRECT answer is:

    A. I, II, III
    B. II, III
    C. II, III, IV
    D. II, III, V
    E. III, V

2. The flaws of Social Darwinism include
    I. a faulty analogy between animal and human society
    II. an historical precedence
    III. ambiguities in being "fit"
    IV. ambiguities in "extinguishing" unfit members of society
    V. there are no flaws
    The CORRECT answer is:

    A. I, III, IV
    B. I, IV
    C. II, III, IV
    D. II, IV
    E. V only

3. One of the social movements that follows as a logical consequence of Social Darwinism is

    A. genocide
    B. racism
    C. sexism
    D. eugenics
    E. utilitarianism

4. The model for Freud's conceptual scheme of the human mind originated with

    A. microbiology
    B. metaphysics
    C. hydraulics
    D. philosophy
    E. none of the above

5. Sartre's theory in BEING AND NOTHINGNESS can best be characterized as
    I. a variety of psychoanalysis
    II. obtuse and obscure
    III. dialectical social theory
    IV. serious, if misguided, speculation
    V. all of the above
    The CORRECT answer is:

    A. I, III
    B. I, III, IV
    C. II, III
    D. III, IV
    E. V only

6. Simone de Beauvoir, in her influential book THE SECOND SEX, draws upon the philosophical theory of

    A. Kierkegaard
    B. Camus
    C. Nietzsche
    D. Freud
    E. Sartre

7. Nietzsche believed that
    I. most people are followers, and only a few can lead
    II. the rules of society apply only to followers, not to the strong
    III. morality is an evil in itself
    IV. only beauty is worth thinking about
    V. all of the above

    The CORRECT answer is:

    A. I, II
    B. I, II, III
    C. II, III, IV
    D. IV *only*
    E. V *only*

8. Schopenhauer's philosophy has been considered a prime example of

    A. optimism
    B. pessimism
    C. abstract idealism
    D. empiricism
    E. none of the above

9. Behavioral psychologists, as strict empiricists, are committed to the claim that
    I. anything that cannot be empirically verified does not exist
    II. only philosophical speculations can produce new knowledge
    III. physical causes are the prime motivators of human behavior
    IV. humans behave much as animals would in the same situation
    V. whatever breathes can be motivated by fear and love

    The CORRECT answer is:

    A. I, II, III
    B. I, III, IV
    C. II, III, IV
    D. III, IV, V
    E. IV, V

10. Utilitarianism supports deterrence in punishment theory because the theory states that

    A. guilty people should be forgiven out of charity
    B. punishing people is one form of causing unhappiness
    C. society does not benefit by retribution
    D. guilt and innocence are too vague to be properly assessed
    E. all of the above

11. The proviso in John Locke's theory that limits how much property a person can own claims that
    I. any goods the individual cannot consume himself belong to others
    II. property owners should not hoard goods until they spoil
    III. a person can accumulate property, as long as there is as much left for others that is as good as what he has
    IV. only if someone pays taxes to a government can he own property
    V. all of the above

    The CORRECT answer is:

A. I, II, III	B. I, III
C. II, III	D. II, III, IV
E. V only	

12. The only two obligations the sovereign has, according to Hobbes, are to

    A. supply prisons and schools
    B. protect citizens from outside attack and provide educations
    C. protect citizens from outside attack and collect taxes
    D. protect citizens from outside attack and enforce contracts
    E. enforce contracts and collect taxes

13. The *primary* justification for the government, according to Hobbes, is that

    A. otherwise we would be miserable and unhappy
    B. it provides social stability by making people keep their word
    C. God has ordained that people be governed by wise rulers
    D. otherwise thieves and murderers would go free
    E. it provides a vindication agent

14. In CIVILIZATION AND ITS DISCONTENTS, Freud argues that
    I. only through Eros does man get what he needs
    II. love has many forms, including hatred
    III. individuals must repress their desires for the sake of society
    IV. society should sacrifice its interests so that individuals can fulfill themselves
    V. there can be no harmony between humans individually and societies in general

    The CORRECT answer is:

A. I, II	B. II, III
C. II, IV	D. III only
E. III, V	

15. Marcuse, in EROS AND CIVILIZATION, disagrees with Freud, in CIVILIZATION AND ITS DISCONTENTS, by saying that

    A. Freud's assumption of egoism and non-benevolence is false
    B. Aristotle was correct in saying that man is a social animal
    C. only through social activity can individuals fulfill themselves
    D. capitalism requires egoistic psychology
    E. all of the above

16. Civil disobedience requires acceptance of punishment because
    I. otherwise the citizens disobeying the law are fomenting revolution
    II. society wants to see rabblerousers put in jail
    III. it is proof that those disobeying the law approve of the system in general
    IV. Thoreau said so
    V. all of the above

    The CORRECT answer is:

A. I, III	B. II, III, IV
C. II, IV	D. III, IV
E. V only	

17. G. E. Moore's "Naturalistic Fallacy" involved the claim that

    A. anyone who adheres to nature's call is committing a fallacy
    B. ethics has nothing to do with the animal kingdom
    C. sociobiology is mistaken
    D. what is good is not the same as what makes people happy
    E. all of the above

18. The surplus labor theory of value claims that
    I. capitalists like surpluses
    II. labor is what makes the world go round
    III. workers lose part of what they labor for
    IV. people only have a right to the fruits of their own labor
    V. all of the above

    The CORRECT answer is:

    A. I, II, III
    B. II, III, IV
    C. III, IV
    D. IV *only*
    E. V *only*

19. The difference between *normative* judgments and *descriptive* ones is that the
    I. former are evaluative
    II. latter are evaluative
    III. former belong to science
    IV. latter belong to science
    V. distinction is important to ethics

    The CORRECT answer is:

    A. I, II, IV
    B. I, IV, V
    C. II, III, V
    D. II, IV, V
    E. IV, V

20. Of the many normative judgments one can make, such as ones including the term *good*, some are NOT moral judgments but rather _____ judgments.
    I. aesthetic
    II. practical
    III. religious
    IV. medical
    V. functional

    The CORRECT answer is:

    A. I, II, III
    B. I, III, V
    C. II, IV, V
    D. I, III, IV, V
    E. all of the above

21. Methodological relativism claims that

    A. though there may be right and wrong, we can never know what it is
    B. there is no right and wrong
    C. right and wrong depend on one's environment
    D. moral judgments originate from customs
    E. all of the above

22. Descriptive relativism claims that
    I. customs vary, but this does not change what is right
    II. customs vary from culture to culture
    III. morality and custom have nothing in common
    IV. mores vary but moral principles can still be true
    V. none of the above
    The CORRECT answer is:

    A. I, III
    B. II, IV
    C. II, III, IV
    D. IV only
    E. V only

23. One crucial issue concerning the morality of abortion is

    A. the separation of church and state
    B. marriage laws
    C. divorce statistics
    D. the humanity of the fetus
    E. government regulation

24. Natural rights are difficult to prove because

    A. people disagree about which ones we have
    B. separating what is natural from what is social is almost impossible
    C. there is a history of Catholic theology behind natural rights
    D. some rights said to be natural are culture-specific
    E. all of the above

25. Positive law theories DISAGREE with natural law theories in that the
    I. former consider official enactments as sufficient to establish law
    II. former believe that law is value-neutral
    III. latter believes that law is value-neutral
    IV. latter believes that law is normative
    V. former denies the obligatoriness of law
    The CORRECT answer is:

    A. I, II, IV
    B. I, III
    C. II, III
    D. II, IV, V
    E. IV, V

26. The view that laws are whatever the sovereign commands is

    A. a natural law theory
    B. a positive law theory
    C. attributable to H. L. A. Hart
    D. attributable to John Austin
    E. none of the above

27. Rehabilitationists, in punishment theory, argue that
    I. only deterrence is a valid consideration when contemplating punishing someone
    II. only the guilty ought to be punished
    III. whether someone deserves punishment or not is irrelevant
    IV. punishment is a crime in itself
    V. all of the above
    The CORRECT answer is:

    A. I, II, III, IV
    B. I, IV
    C. II, III
    D. III, IV
    E. V *only*

28. You are insane under the law if you
    I. do not know the law
    II. act very strangely in public
    III. do not know what you are doing
    IV. do not care what others think about you
    V. do not know right from wrong
    The CORRECT answer is:

    A. I *only*
    B. II, III
    C. II, III, IV
    D. III, IV
    E. III, V

29. Lon Fuller, the philosopher of jurisprudence, DISAGREES with Hart in that
    I. Fuller believes the law is normative while Hart does not
    II. Hart believes the law is normative while Fuller does not
    III. Fuller follows the natural law tradition
    IV. Hart follows the natural law tradition
    V. Fuller follows the positivist tradition
    The CORRECT answer is:

    A. I *only*
    B. I, II
    C. I, III
    D. I, IV, V
    E. III, V

30. THE CONCEPT OF LAW, the famous book of jurisprudential theory, was written by

    A. Oliver Wendell Holmes
    B. John Austin
    C. H. L. A. Hart
    D. Lon Fuller
    E. none of the above

31. In philosophy of law, there is a dispute as to whether or not rules are
    I. valid
    II. sound
    III. normative
    IV. generalized
    V. stipulative
    The CORRECT answer is:

    A. I, II, III, IV
    B. II, IV, V
    C. II, V
    D. III, IV, V
    E. IV, V

32. The *fundamental* reason for determining the legitimacy of law is that

   A. it is coercive
   B. otherwise we will not obey laws
   C. judges require it
   D. scholars love to do it
   E. all of the above

33. John Stuart Mill's criterion for limiting the law's reach states that the law has no business with an individual's self-regarding actions. Problems with this include that

   A. some individuals act destructively
   B. it is difficult to act so as only to affect oneself
   C. some individuals are self-destructive
   D. police ignore Mill's criterion anyway
   E. all of the above

34. One of the MOST important issues in philosophy of law is whether or not

   A. we ought to have any laws at all
   B. laws are morally binding
   C. laws ought to legislate morality
   D. people ought to be expected to know the law
   E. we have enough laws

35. Problems with deterrence theory include
   I. the fact that it does not work
   II. the fact that it ignores what people deserve
   III. its utilitarian foundation
   IV. its humaneness
   V. its lack of humaneness

   The CORRECT answer is:

   A. I, II, III, IV   B. I, II, V
   C. I, III, V   D. II, III, V
   E. II, IV

36. A MAJOR epistemological issue discussed in Plato's THEATETUS concerns

   A. whether or not humans wish to have knowledge
   B. whether or not knowledge is even possible
   C. why it is difficult to discuss knowledge philosophically
   D. the difference between knowledge and true opinion or belief
   E. the nature of love

37. John Austin's "Descriptive Fallacy" states that

   A. we are mistaken if we think we can describe reality
   B. a person's claims to knowledge are always doubtful
   C. the claim "I know" does not describe anything
   D. the claim "I know" does describe something
   E. descriptions are always wrong

38. A MAJOR issue in theory of action is

   A. how many descriptions accurately apply to the "same" action
   B. whether or not we act at all
   C. whether or not intentions are necessary for action
   D. how we go from a thought to an action
   E. all of the above

39. Certain kinds of statements, according to John Austin, DO something, such as when "I promise" puts us under an obligation. These are

   A. exclamations   B. interrogatives
   C. performatives   D. indicatives
   E. subjunctives

40. In contemporary epistemology, an issue hotly debated is

   A. that concerning innate ideas
   B. whether or not God knows ahead of time what we will do
   C. whether or not we need to know metaphysics before epistemology
   D. whether knowledge is directly or indirectly given
   E. none of the above

41. The school of thought MOST OPPOSED to empiricism in epistemology is

   A. intuitionism   B. physicalism
   C. determinism   D. materialism
   E. none of the above

42. Universal ethical egoism can be stated as:

   A. Everyone ought to act in the self-interest of one agent
   B. I ought to act in my own self-interest
   C. Everyone ought to act in his own self-interest
   D. Everyone always acts in his own self-interest
   E. None of the above

43. An act that is *prima facie* wrong, such as killing, may be

   A. actually right   B. still wrong
   C. unjustifiable   D. justified
   E. none of the above

44. The principle in ethics that states that no one should make an exception of himself with respect to morality can be called a

   A. principle of fairness
   B. principle of goodness
   C. principle of universalization
   D. logical principle
   E. all of the above

45. "A Nazi SS guard comes to the door of a German in 1939 and demands to know whether there are Jews hidden there. Mrs. X has hidden 3 Jews in her basement; is it right for her to lie?"
    The philosopher who believes Mrs. X should tell the truth is

    A. Moore
    B. Mill
    C. Bentham
    D. Kant
    E. Sartre

46. The philosophical phenomenon of intentionality was originated by

    A. Hegel
    B. Marx
    C. Sartre
    D. Montague
    E. Husserl

47. Epiphenomenalism is the theory in philosophy of mind that states that

    A. the body and the mind both affect each other
    B. bodies and minds never affect each other
    C. we only really have a mind
    D. we only really have a body
    E. only the body affects the mind, not the reverse

48. One central issue in philosophy of mind is

    A. analyzing love and hate
    B. figuring out which psychological system is correct
    C. determining what the "self" is
    D. determining the nature of ultimate reality
    E. analyzing epistemological criteria

49. "What is left over if I subtract the fact that my arm goes up from the fact that I raise my arm?"
    This famous modern philosophical problem comes from

    A. Russell
    B. Strawson
    C. Austin
    D. Wittgenstein
    E. Moore

50. Gilbert Ryle's "ghost in the machine" criticism challenged the view that

    A. computers can think
    B. volitions are necessary for actions
    C. our thoughts are clear
    D. most people think at all
    E. all of the above

KEY (CORRECT ANSWERS)

1. B	11. A	21. A	31. D	41. A
2. A	12. D	22. B	32. A	42. C
3. D	13. B	23. D	33. B	43. D
4. C	14. E	24. E	34. C	44. C
5. A	15. E	25. A	35. B	45. D
6. E	16. A	26. D	36. D	46. E
7. A	17. D	27. B	37. C	47. E
8. B	18. C	28. E	38. E	48. C
9. B	19. B	29. C	39. C	49. D
10. B	20. E	30. C	40. D	50. B

EXAMINATION SECTION
TEST 1

DIRECTIONS: Each question or incomplete statement is followed by several suggested answers or completions. Select the one that BEST answers the question or completes the statement. *PRINT THE LETTER OF THE CORRECT ANSWER IN THE SPACE AT THE RIGHT.*

1. In Plato's APOLOGY, Socrates
   I. apologizes to the people of Athens for his misbehavior
   II. defends himself against various charges
   III. participates in a typical Platonic dialogue
   IV. is found guilty
   V. All of the above
   The CORRECT answer is:

   A. I, II   B. II, III   C. III, IV   D. II, IV   E. V only

   1._____

2. Socrates was not afraid of death because
   I. he was satisfied with the worldly success he had already attained
   II. the soul is immortal
   III. he didn't know enough about it
   IV. he was sick of his poverty-stricken life
   V. None of the above
   The CORRECT answer is:

   A. I, II   B. II, III   C. III, IV   D. IV only   E. V only

   2._____

3. In both the ancient and the modern sense of the word, "sophistry" means

   A. manipulating arguments to prove a point
   B. accepting a fee for supplying arguments
   C. having knowledge or wisdom
   D. an occult science
   E. all of the above

   3._____

4. The crimes Socrates was accused of included the following:

   A. Being an atheist
   B. Creating his own gods
   C. Corrupting the youth
   D. Defeating good arguments with bad ones
   E. All of the above

   4._____

5. The dialogues of Plato were
   I. actually written by Socrates
   II. written by Plato but used all of Socrates' ideas
   III. dramatic inventions created by Plato alone
   IV. semi-historical accounts of conversations in Athens at the time
   V. unrelated to the political events of the time
   The CORRECT answer is:

   A. I, II, III   B. III, V   C. II, IV   D. II, III, V   E. I, IV

   5._____

6. Crito tried to persuade Socrates to escape from prison because
    A. people would think Plato abandoned his old friend Socrates
    B. there was plenty of money rrom foreigners to bribe the guards
    C. Socrates' verdict and sentence were unjust
    D. he had a moral obligation to his family
    E. All of the above

7. Socrates refused to escape from prison because
    I. his act of disobedience would destroy the laws of the land
    II. he owed his life to the state
    III. he thought he would be caught
    IV. there was no other place to go
    V. by staying in Athens, he had tacitly agreed to obey the law
    The CORRECT answer is:

    A. I, II, V   B. II, III, V   C. I, III, IV   D. III, IV, V
    E. I, II, III, V

8. Socrates was sentenced to die by means of

    A. hanging   B. being drawn and quar-   C. drowning
                          tered
    D. drinking hemlock   E. being beheaded

9. Socrates' famous quotations include:
    I. "Know thyself"
    II. "The unexamined life is not worth living"
    III. "I think, therefore I am"
    IV. "What is important is not to live, but to live well."
    V. "Everything that is true or real is eternal"
    The CORRECT answer is:

    A. I, II   B. I, II, III   C. I, II, III, IV   D. I, II, IV, V
    E. All of the above

10. The Socratic method involves

    A. challenging authorities   B. playing devil's advocate
    C. asking questions   D. defending unorthodox opinions
    E. close scrutiny of famous philosophi-
       cal publications

11. In philosophy, an idealist is someone who
    I. is optimistic about the future
    II. pursues abstract, not concrete, truth
    III. rejects the scientific method as unreliable
    IV. holds a metaphysical view opposed to materialism
    V. values ideas over physical objects
    The CORRECT answer is:

    A. I, II   B. II, III   C. I, II, III   D. I, III, V   E. II, III, IV, V

12. The jury at Socrates' trial was composed of
    I. twelve peers
    II. over one hundred citizens of Athens
    III. both men and women, young and old
    IV. both friends and enemies
    V. only propertied aristocrats
    The CORRECT answer is:

    A. II, III, IV   B. I, III, V   C. II, IV, V   D. III, IV, V
    E. I, III

13. Plato's famous THEORY OF FORMS concerned
    I. how citizens appeared to the rulers of the state
    II. epistemological issues
    III. universal truths
    IV. Socrates' pursuit of the truth
    V. all of the above
    The CORRECT answer is:

    A. I, II, III   B. I, V   C. I, IV, V   D. II, III, V   E. II, III, IV

14. Strictly speaking, the word "philosophy" means

    A. study of knowledge   B. the thought process
    C. wise old men   D. love of wisdom
    E. pondering profound problems

15. The Ontological Argument tries to prove
    I. that reality is not real
    II. that ontology is the true root of metaphysics
    III. that God exists
    IV. that the meaning of terms is sufficient evidence for existence
    V. none of the above
    The CORRECT answer is:

    A. I, II   B. II, III   C. III, IV   D. IV, V   E. I, V

16. The following statement,
    If there are more trees in the world than there are leaves on any one tree, and no trees have no leaves, then there are at least two trees with the same number of leaves, is:

    A. *False*, because it is highly improbable
    B. *True*, because it is highly probable
    C. *False*, because the last claim is unrelated to the first two claims
    D. *True*, because 0=0
    E. *True*, by definition

17. Empirical statements are
    I. a posteriori claims
    II. provable through observable evidence
    III. incapable of being 100% true
    IV. never certain
    V. essential to science
    The CORRECT answer is:

| A. I, II | B. I, II, III | C. I, IV, V | D. I, II, III, IV |

E. All of the above

18. A priori statements are

    A. true (or false) by definition
    B. invariably 100% true or false
    C. provable through logical analysis
    D. reliant upon the meaning of terms
    E. all of the above

19. Descartes's famous claim, *"Cogito, ergo sum,"* means:

    A. "Do unto others as you would have them do unto you"
    B. "I am, therefore I think."
    C. "I think, therefore I am."
    D. Thinking is the only true source of truth
    E. all of the above

20. Descrates's *"methodological doubt"* consisted of

    A. wondering whether the chair he sat on was real
    B. wondering how we ever know whether we are dreaming
    C. casting off all claims that cannot be proved 100% true
    D. temporarily believing that life is an illusion
    E. all of the above

21. Some of the examples used by Descartes to justify his method include

    | A. hallucinations | B. dreams | C. balls of wax |
    | D. God may really be an Evil Demon | E. all of the above | |

22. The Ontological Argument is

    A. quite different from the Cosmological Argument
    B. originally the ingenious idea of a priest
    C. a good example of an a priori argument
    D. short, elegant, and abstract
    E. all of the above

23. Some of the flaws in the Ontological Argument are that
    I. its crucial definition is ambiguous
    II. it assumes that existence is a predicate
    III. only religious people could possibly be persuaded by it
    IV. it requires a knowledge of mathematics to understand it
    V. a counter-argument refutes it easily

    The CORRECT answer is:

    | A. I, III | B. I, II, III | C. II, III, IV | D. III, IV |

    E. I, II, V

24. Metaphysics is
    I. the study of ontology
    II. the basis of epistemology
    III. a field in philosophy that tries to answer the question, *"What is real?"*
    IV. an analysis of physics
    V. studied by all philosophers of any stature
    The CORRECT answer is:

    A. I, III   B. I, IV   C. II, IV   D. IV, V   E. III, IV

25. Logic is
    I. the study of a priori statements
    II. something invented by Aristotle
    III. concerned with concrete, empirical reality
    IV. concerned with abstract relations
    V. all of the above
    The CORRECT answer is:

    A. I, III   B. I, II, IV   C. I, II, III   D. III, IV   E. v *only*

26. A set of statements, one of which is a conclusion and the other(s) of which is a(are) premise(s), is a description of

    A. a syllogism   B. an argument   C. only valid arguments
    D. only sound arguments   E. all of the above

27. Epistemology concerns
    I. examining metaphysical claims to see whether they are true
    II. the analysis of logical arguments
    III. substantiating claims of knowledge
    IV. physical facts
    V. human beliefs
    The CORRECT answer is:

    A. I, III, V   B. I, II, IV   C. I, II, III   D. III, V   E. II, V

28. *"If p, then q; p, therefore q."* This is an example of
    I. Modus Ponens
    II. Modus Tollens
    III. invalid reasoning
    IV. valid reasoning
    V. calculus
    The CORRECT answer is:

    A. I, II   B. III, IV   C. I, IV   D. III, V   E. I, V

29. The pantheist believes
    I. that there is only one God
    II. that there are many gods
    III. that both animate and inanimate nature are part of God's nature
    IV. there is nowhere God cannot be found
    V. all of the above
    The CORRECT answer is:

A. I, III B. II, III C. III, IV D. I, II, III
E. V only

30. Some of the 10 terms of predication for Aristotle are:
    I. quantity and quality
    II. passivity and activity
    III. place and position
    IV. time
    V. none of the above
    The CORRECT answer is:

    A. I, III, V B. I, II, III, IV C. II, III, IV
    D. I, IV E. V only

31. A deductive argument is one in which
    I. all the premises can be proved to be true
    II. the conclusion is true if the premises are true
    III. the proof lies in mathematical relations
    IV. the conclusion it establishes is highly probable
    V. the conclusion is either true or false
    The CORRECT answer is:

    A. I, III B. II, III C. I, II, III D. II, III, IV
    E. II, III, V

32. Inductive arguments differ from deductive arguments in that
    I. the former establish a conclusion with certainty, not probability
    II. the latter establish a conclusion with certainty, not probability
    III. the former may have true premises and a false conclusion
    IV. empirical evidence is relevant to the former and not to the latter
    V. empirical evidence is relevant to the latter and not to the former
    The CORRECT answer is:

    A. II, III, IV B. I, II, III C. III, IV, V D. IV, V
    E. II, III, V

33. The conclusion of an inductive argument

    A. may be established by several premises whose number is unlimited
    B. is fortified by an increasing number of substantiating cases
    C. is weakened by a lack of empirical evidence
    D. is typically arrived at by enumerative induction
    E. All of the above

34. A valid argument
    I. has true premises and a false conclusion
    II. has true premises
    III. has a conclusion that follows from the premises
    IV. requires some experience with what it is about to prove it
    V. is the same as a sound argument
    The CORRECT answer is:

    A. I, II B. III, IV C. III only D. III, V E. I, IV, V

35. A sound argument
    I. has true premises
    II. has true premises and a false conclusion
    III. is valid and has true premises
    IV. has false premises and a true conclusion
    V. always persuades an audience
    The CORRECT answer is:

    A. i, ii   B. ii, IV   C. iii, V   D. i, ii, iii   E. i, iii

36. "There are no purple swans" is an example of a(n)

    A. typical philosopher's puzzle
    B. universalization
    C. generalization
    D. existential claim
    E. negative existential universal

37. "There are no purple swans" is a

    A. statement that is obviously false
    B. statement that one could prove, though with difficulty
    C. statement that cannot be proved
    D. good way to begin a conversation
    E. statement that is obviously true

38. An analogy is a(n)

    A. literary metaphor
    B. form of deductive argument
    C. comparison used to prove a point
    D. simile
    E. All of the above

39. A non sequitur is a(n)
    I. statement that follows deductively from a premise
    II. statement that does not follow deductively from a premise
    III. statement that does not follow from the previous statement
    IV. statement that contradicts itself
    V. easy way to make people laugh
    The CORRECT answer is:

    A. I, II   B. I, II, III   C. III, IV   D. III, V   E. I, III, V

40. An "equivocation" is a fallacy in which
    I. the terms being used are vague
    II. the terms being used are obscure and undefined
    III. there is more than one meaning to one or more terms
    IV. the central problem is invalidity
    V. All of the above
    The CORRECT answer is:

    A. I only   B. I, II, III   C. IV, V   D. III, V   E. III, IV

41. If half the slots on a roulette wheel are red and the other half are black, and if 25 times in a row the ball falls in a red slot, *then* the chances
    I. are very high that the 26th ball will fall in a black slot
    II. are better that the 26th ball will fall in a black slot
    III. that the 26th ball will fall in a black slot are lower than they were
    IV. that the 26th ball will fall in a black slot are 50-50
    V. that the 26th ball will fall in a black slot are the same as for the previous 25 instances

    The CORRECT answer is:

    A. I, IV, V   B. I, II, III   C. IV, V   D. III, IV   E. I, V

42. Medieval philosophy was largely concerned with
    I. discussing the morality of torture devices
    II. justifying the divine right of kings
    III. theology
    IV. studying Plato
    V. translating Plato from ancient Greek into Latin

    The CORRECT answer is:

    A. I, II, III   B. I, II, III, IV   C. II, .III, IV, V   D. I, III, IV, V
    E. III, IV, V

43. In all likelihood, ancient cultures *first* discovered order in the universe by
    I. developing complex mathematical systems
    II. establishing stable political regimes that encouraged abstract research
    III. observations made while hunting for food
    IV. observations of the uniformity of the stars
    V. researching religious documents

    The CORRECT answer is:

    A. I, II   B. II, III   C. III, IV   D. IV, V   E. II, IV

44. The following famous statement, *"All humans by nature desire to know,"* was *first* stated by

    A. Plato   B. Saint Augustine   C. Aristotle
    D. Freud   E. Democritus

45. A *reductio ad absurdum* argument is one that
    I. inductively proves what it sets out to prove
    II. deductively proves what it sets out to prove
    III. deductively proves the opposite of what it set out to prove
    IV. succeeds only if it results in a condtradiction
    V. is used frequently and very effectively

    The CORRECT answer is:

    A. I, II, III   B. III, IV, V   C. II, III, IV   D. I, III, V
    E. I, III

46. *"Social Darwinism"* is a theory about society developed by

    A. Freud   B. Darwin   C. John Stuart Mill
    D. Herbert Spencer   E. none of the above

47. What is TRUE of the following statement: *Human society benefits by the extinction of its unfit members?"* It
    I. *relies upon* an analogy between biological survival and social relations
    II. *accurately describes* current social systems
    III. *presupposes* that what is biologically good is morally good
    IV. *confuses* natural laws with moral laws
    V. *justifies* continued exploitation of the sick and the poor
    The CORRECT answer is:

    A. I, III, V B. I, II, III, IV C. II, IV, V
    D. I, III, IV, V E. II, III, IV, V

48. The *fundamental* issue in political philosophy is

    A. justice
    B. governmental regulations
    C. the relationship of the church and the state
    D. courts and the law
    E. democratic theories of representation

49. *First and foremost,* social justice concerns

    A. equal opportunity
    B. reasonable legislation
    C. a good court system
    D. the distribution of economic wealth
    E. formal rules of election

50. A tautology is a(n)
    I. contradictory statement
    II. invalid argument
    III. true statement
    IV. a priori statement
    V. statement that is true by definition
    The CORRECT answer is:

    A. III, IV, V B. I, II, III C. I, III, V D. II, IV, V
    E. None of the above

KEY (CORRECT ANSWERS)

1. D	11. E	21. E	31. E	41. C
2. B	12. C	22. E	32. A	42. C
3. A	13. E	23. E	33. E	43. E
4. E	14. D	24. A	34. B	44. C
5. C	15. C	25. B	35. D	45. B
6. E	16. E	26. B	36. E	46. D
7. A	17. E	27. D	37. C	47. D
8. D	18. E	28. C	38. C	48. A
9. D	19. E	29. C	39. D	49. D
10. C	20. C	30. B	40. E	50. A

TEST 2

DIRECTIONS: Each question or incomplete statement is followed by several suggested answers or completions. Select the one that BEST answers the question or completes the statement. *PRINT THE LETTER OF THE CORRECT ANSWER IN THE SPACE AT THE RIGHT.*

1. Machiavelli is credited with

   A. developing the first theory of political science
   B. establishing the ways and means of obtaining political power
   C. using his theoretical knowledge to gain a position of political power
   D. challenging religious values
   E. All of the above

1.____

2. In THE PRINCE, Machiavelli *basically*
   I. formulates abstract principles of political philosophy
   II. uses anecdotes from Italian history to prove his point
   III. tries to show how valuable political experience is to members of the nobility
   IV. draws upon the accepted theories of his day to draw attention to himself
   V. offers advice to would-be rulers

   The CORRECT combination is:

   A. I, II, V   B. I, IV, V   C. I, II, III   D. II, III
   E. II, III, V

2.____

3. Some of the *main* points Machiavelli makes are:
   I. Members of society cannot tolerate freedom
   II. Rulers do not need to appear honest or generous; all they need is power
   III. Political power depends primarily upon talent and ability in a ruler
   IV. Brutality and ruthlessness are sometimes justified if done for the benefit of society
   V. People seek to maximize their own self-interest

   The CORRECT combination is:

   A. I, II, III   B. III, IV, V   C. II, III, V   D. I, III, IV
   E. II, III, IV

3.____

4. If Machiavelli's advice could be captured in one word, it would be

   A. power   B. control   C. fortune   D. ability
   E. prudence

4.____

5. Some scholars have challenged Machiavelli's status as the first political scientist on the grounds that:
   I. His morality was simply too repulsive to gain academic respectability
   II. No scholarly work done before 1920 can possibly be legitimate
   III. Historical anecdotes are no substitute for statistical research
   IV. He changes his principles frequently, depending upon the situation he is discussing
   V. His primary purpose in writing THE PRINCE was to get a job

   The CORRECT combination is:

   A. I, II   B. I, II, III   C. I, II, III, IV   D. I, III, V
   E. All of the above

5.____

6. Thomas Hobbes' *primary* purpose in his book THE LEVIATHAN (1651) was

   A. to show how human nature and society fulfilled God's wishes
   B. to prove that human nature is basically egoistic
   C. to illustrate how mechanistic psychology can help substantiate political theory
   D. to justify the citizen's obligation to the state
   E. All of the above

7. In Hobbes' *"state of nature"* theory, humans are, without laws and government,
   I. energetic and cooperative
   II. envious and acquisitive
   III. selfish and greedy
   IV. lonely and insecure
   V. equal in their ability to kill one another

   The CORRECT combination is:

   A. II, III, IV, V B. I, II, III, IV C. I, III, IV, V
   D. I, II, III, V   E. All of the above

8. Egoism is a theory that states
   I. everyone *always* seeks to maximize his/her self-interest
   II. everyone *usually* seeks to maximize his/her self-interest
   III. everyone seeks his/her own interest, whether or not it is at another's expense
   IV. everyone seeks to increase his own interest primarily to thwart others
   V. any apparently altruistic act is really self-interested

   The CORRECT combination is:

   A. I, II   B. I, V   C. I, III, V   D. I, II, III   E. II, III, IV

9. Altruism is the theory that states that
   I. everyone always seeks to maximize others' interest
   II. everyone seeks to act in his/her own interest as well as in others'
   III. not all actions are done in order to maximize the self-interest of the agent
   IV. egoism and altruism are not mutually exclusive
   V. egoism is false

   The CORRECT combination is:

   A. I, II, III, IV   B. II, III, IV, V   C. I, III, V   D. II, III, IV
   E. All of the above

10. Since life in the *"state of nature,"* according to Hobbes, is *"nasty, brutish, and short,"* a government is necessary in order to

    A. monopolize coercive power into one agency
    B. enforce agreements and contracts
    C. defend the country against outside attack
    D. give people a reason not to maximize self-interest
    E. All of the above

11. Hobbes is a nominalist because
    I. he claims that people are egoistic
    II. he uses scientific reasoning to establish his conclusions
    III. he believes that there is no justice or goodness in nature
    IV. only the state can create rights
    V. past experience is not a guide for judging actions
    The CORRECT combination is:

    A. I, III, IV B. I, II, III C. II, IV D. III, IV
    E. IV, V

12. A hedonist is one who believes that

    A. love makes the world go round
    B. pleasure is the highest good
    C. only power brings success
    D. truth is always more persuasive than falsity
    E. None of the above

13. Physicalism is a
    I. variety of materialism
    II. variety of idealism
    III. theory that identifies causes and physical objects
    IV. view that reduces psychology to physiology
    V. theory that claims that every effect has a cause
    The CORRECT combination is:

    A. I, II B. I, II, III C. I, III, IV, V D. II, III, IV, V
    E. All of the above

14. Empiricism is a theory that states that
    I. anything that cannot be observed is non-existent
    II. human behavior can only be explained through the scientific principles of cause and effect
    III. mental images and ideas are only faint copies of physical sensations
    IV. thinking makes it so
    V. observation is the only test of truth
    The CORRECT combination is:

    A. All of the above B. I, II, III, V C. I, II, III, IV
    D. I, III, V E. II, III, V

15. Determinism is a theory that states:
    I. Human efforts can change the world
    II. Every human action can be traced to a physical cause
    III. Your thoughts about what you do have no effect on your actions
    IV. There is no such thing as free will
    V. People are basically egoistic
    The CORRECT combination is:

    A. I, III, V B. I, II, III C. II, III, V D. I, III, IV
    E. II, III, IV

16. Max Weber, an early sociologist, is well-known for
    I. using modern methodologies in his field
    II. showing the connection between Puritan Protestantism and capitalism
    III. developing statistical techniques in social science
    IV. including values in his research and findings
    V. his theories about political power
    The CORRECT combination is:

    A. I, II, III   B. II, III, IV   C. I, II, IV   D. III, IV, V
    E. I, III, V

17. A humanist is someone who
    I. disbelieves in God
    II. promotes ethical values as the most important
    III. emphasizes the power of humans to do good
    IV. encourages active participation in life
    V. takes advantage of findings of modern social sciences
    The CORRECT combination is:

    A. I, II   B. III, IV   C. I, III, V   D. I, II, III, IV
    E. II, III, IV, V

18. A necessary condition is one that
    I. helps reach a conclusion
    II. must obtain for the result
    III. is enough by itself to bring about a result
    IV. never found for most situations in life
    V. cannot be omitted without losing the result
    The CORRECT combination is:

    A. I, II   B. II, III   C. III, IV   D. III, V   E. II, V

19. A sufficient condition is one that

    A. is enough by itself to bring about a result
    B. needs other conditions to satisfy all requirements
    C. is rarely found in most circumstances
    D. is optional for a given conclusion
    E. is usually equivalent for that which it is a condition of

20. Descriptive statements differ from normative ones in that the
    I. *former* include value judgments while the latter do not
    II. *latter* include value judgments while the former do not
    III. *former* are co-extensive with ordinary empirical claims
    IV. *latter* use some word such as "good" or "bad"
    V. *former* are morally neutral
    The CORRECT combination is:

    A. I, V   B. II, V   C. III, IV   D. IV, V   E. I, III, V

21. A presupposition of an argument is
    I. a logical conclusion to the premises
    II. a hidden premise
    III. an assumption underlying one or all the premises
    IV. useful to identify when analyzing the argument
    V. All of the above
    The CORRECT combination is:

    A. I, II   B. II, III   C. II, IV   D. III, IV   E. V

22. Buridan, a medieval logician, had an Ass (donkey) that was a rational agent, i.e., it sought to maximize its own self-interest. Placed equidistant between two entirely identical piles of hay, the donkey (given the above conditions) would decide to

    A. randomly choose either of the two piles of hay
    B. flip a coin to choose which to begin eating
    C. starve to death in a paralysis of decision
    D. first go to one pile and eat, then to the next
    E. give up on rationality

23. A *universal* statement differs from a *general* statement in that the
    I. *former* covers all instances while the latter does not
    II. *latter* covers all instances while the former does not
    III. *former* can be refuted by a single counter-example
    IV. *latter* can be refuted by a single counter-example
    V. *latter* constitutes much of science
    The CORRECT combination is:

    A. I, III   B. I, V   C. I, III, V   D. II, III, V   E. III, V

24. Fatalism is a theory that claims that
    I. God has prearranged all of our lives down to the last detail
    II. everything that happens was meant to happen
    III. nothing we do will change the future in any way
    IV. people should not be held responsible for what happens in life
    V. only scientific investigation explains reality
    The CORRECT combination is:

    A. I, II   B. II, III   C. III, IV   D. II, III, IV
    E. II, III, V

25. Aristotle was renowned for his philosophical methodology which was

    A. characterized by its empirical nature
    B. in stark contrast to Platonic philosophy
    C. frequently in harmony with common sense
    D. a forerunner of the techniques of modern scientific method
    E. All of the above

26. Teleological theories in ethics are ones that
    I. emphasize the nature of the act in question for morality
    II. concern the consequences or outcomes of an act for morality
    III. are sometimes called consequentialist theories
    IV. require an in-depth knowledge of human nature
    V. depend upon ordinary common sense notions about right and wrong
    The CORRECT combination is:

    A. II, III, V　　B. I, II, III　　C. I, III, IV　　D. I, IV, V
    E. II, III

27. Deontological theories in ethics are ones that
    I. are not teleological
    II. are not consequentialist
    III. are consequentialist but not teleological
    IV. are teleological but not consequentialist
    V. emphasize the nature of an act for moral evaluation
    The CORRECT combination is:

    A. I, III　　B. I, V　　C. II, IV　　D. I, III, IV　　E. I, III, V

28. Kant's ethics relied heavily upon
    I. human capacity for reason
    II. past experience of immoral and moral behavior
    III. taking into account differences in people and situations
    IV. making moral judgments universal
    V. figuring out the consequences of actions
    The CORRECT combination is:

    A. I, V　　B. I, IV　　C. II, IV　　D. III, IV　　E. I, IV, V

29. The Categorical Imperative, according to Kant, stated that

    A. autonomy is an important moral prerequisite
    B. everyone should be willing to have others do as they do
    C. as long as a person does what is right, motives are irrelevant
    D. orders should be followed categorically
    E. None of the above

30. The following are TRUE of Kantian ethics:
    I. It is a deontological theory
    II. It is a teleological theory
    III. Its foundation lies in empirical fact
    IV. Its foundation lies in a priori reasoning
    V. It is deterministic
    The CORRECT combination is:

    A. I, III　　B. II, III　　C. II, IV　　D. I, IV　　E. I only

31. If some types of behavior are part of human nature,
    I. it is still understandable if some people do not exhibit it
    II. it is not understandable if some people do not exhibit it
    III. if some people do not exhibit it, it is not part of human nature
    IV. it is universally found
    V. All of the above
    The CORRECT combination is:

    A. V only B. II, III C. III, IV D. II, III, IV
    E. I, II, III

32. Some *primary* elements in Kantian ethics are
    I. having a good will
    II. justifying paternalistic behavior
    III. preserving autonomy for the individual
    IV. treating people as an end, not as a means
    V. looking out for the self-interests of others
    The CORRECT combination is:

    A. I, IV B. II, IV C. III, IV D. I, III, IV
    E. I, III, V

33. The principle of Universalization requires that
    I. no person make an exception of himself/herself in morality
    II. what is required of one person in a given situation is required of any other similar person in a relevantly similar situation
    III. moral rules apply equally to all
    IV. no one should evaluate each situation on its own merits
    V. everyone should evaluate each situation on its own merits
    The CORRECT combination is:

    A. I, II, III B. III, IV, V C. II, III, IV, V D. I, II, III, IV
    E. All of the above

34. Concepts that have no place in Kantian ethics are:
    I. duty
    II. intentions
    III. motivation
    IV. consequences
    V. relativism
    The CORRECT combination is:

    A. I, II, III B. II, III, IV C. IV, V D. I only
    E. III only

35. Concepts that are *crucial* to Kantian ethics are:
    I. duty
    II. intentions
    III. motivation
    IV. consequences
    V. relativism
    The CORRECT combination is:

    A. I, II, III B. II, III, IV C. I, II D. I, III
    E. II, III, IV

36. Relativism states
    I. nothing precisely
    II. that everyone has different moral beliefs so that it is impossible to say for sure what is right or wrong
    III. that what is right in one place is wrong in another
    IV. that it is usually clear what is right and what is wrong
    V. there is no such thing as right and wrong
    The CORRECT combination is:

    A. I, II   B. I, II, III   C. I, II, III, IV   D. III, V
    E. I, II, III, V

37. Popular versions of relativistic ethics include the following sorts of claims:

    A. "Who are you to judge?"
    B. "Right and wrong depend upon the culture one is in"
    C. "No one ought to judge others"
    D. "It is wrong to make moral judgments"
    E. All of the above

38. The following claim(s) of relativism is(are) logically fallacious :

    A. "Who are you to judge?"
    B. "Right and wrong depend upon the culture one is in"
    C. "No one ought to judge others"
    D. "It is wrong to make moral judgments"
    E. All of the above

39. Emotivism is a moral theory that states
    I. that moral judgments are based on intuition
    II. that how much a person wants a certain consequence of an action determines whether it is right or not
    III. that morality is simply a matter of how a person feels
    IV. that moral judgements like "Stealing is wrong" are precisely like statements like "I like chocolate ice cream"
    V. All of the above
    The CORRECT combination is:

    A. I, III   B. II, III   C. I, III, IV   D. III, IV
    E. None of the above

40. Cognitivism is the theory that states that moral judgments
    I. are emotional expressions
    II. cannot be proved one way or the other
    III. are capable of being true or false
    IV. are provable by standard empirical evidence
    V. are provable by analytical reasoning
    The CORRECT combination is:

    A. I, II, III   B. II, III, IV   C. III, IV   D. III, IV, V
    E. IV, V

41. John Stuart Mill upheld utilitarianism in
    I. precisely the same way his father, James Mill, did
    II. precisely the same way Jeremy Bentham, its founder, did
    III. a different way from James Mill
    IV. a different way from Jeremy Bentham
    V. an extensively revised version
    The CORRECT combination is:

    A. I, III, IV   B. II, III, IV   C. III, V   D. III, IV
    E. IV, V

42. Utilitarianism is a theory that states that
    I. a person's intentions must be taken into account when judging his/her action
    II. a person's intentions need not be taken into account when judging his/her action
    III. actions should be useful before they are virtuous
    IV. efficiency is the highest moral goal
    V. utility is the sole principle of right conduct
    The CORRECT combination is:

    A. I, II   B. II, IV   C. I, II, V   D. II, V   E. II, III, V

43. Jeremy Bentham's *"hedonistic calculus"* prescribed that everyone should
    I. try to figure out how satisfied others will be by a particular act to determine whether it is right
    II. determine for himself/herself whether an act will make him/her happy
    III. evaluate intellectual pursuits differently from sensual ones
    IV. total up the different utilities of everyone to find out which act is morally obligatory
    V. total up the different utilities of only those involved to find out which act is morally obligatory
    The CORRECT combination is:

    A. II, III   B. II, IV   C. IV, V   D. II, IV, V
    E. II, V

44. According to Bentham, utility can be determined by
    I. each person using a *cardinal* scale for a number revealing his/her level of happiness
    II. each person using an *ordinal* scale for determining his/her level of happiness
    III. *objective* evidence concerning what is ultimately good for people
    IV. *subjectively* evidence concerning what people like
    V. using past experience as a reliable guide
    The CORRECT combination is:

    A. I, IV, V   B. II, III, IV   C. III, IV, V   D. I, II   E. IV, V

45. An action that is *prima facie* right is one that
    I. conforms with a moral rule or principle
    II. violates a moral rule or principle
    III. is the kind of action that harms people
    IV. may be found later to be unjustified
    V. is the kind of action that harms no one
    The CORRECT combination is:

    A. I, IV, V   B. II, IV, V   C. I, III, V   D. I, II   E. IV, V

46. Some actions are intrinsically wrong.
    I. Utilitarian theory *affirms* this
    II. Utilitarian theory *denies* this
    III. Deontological theory *affirms* this
    IV. Deontological theory *denies* this
    V. Emotivism *denies* this
    The CORRECT combination is:

    A. I, III, V   B. II, IV, V   C. II, III, V   D. I, III   E. III, V

47. Mill's revisions of Bentham's utilitarian included
    I. *widening* the role of "pleasure" to include non-sensual things
    II. *reducing* the role of consequences in making moral decisions
    III. *challenging* Bentham's dictum that "Pushpin is as good as poetry"
    IV. *agreeing with* Bentham's dictum that "Pushpin is as good as poetry"
    V. *claiming* that "Better a Socrates dissatisfied than a pig satisfied"
    The CORRECT combination is:

    A. II, IV, V   B. II, III, V   C. I, III, V   D. I, V   E. I, III

48. Mill corrected a serious flaw in utilitarian theory by adding the following phrase or statement to standard utilitarianism:

    A. "for the greatest number"
    B. "Right actions maximize the happiness of the agent and those affected by the act"
    C. "with good intentions"
    D. "The ultimate goal of morality is to promote the greatest good"
    E. "in God we trust"

49. Act-utilitarianism states that
    I. moral rules should be made concerning typical actions people perform every day
    II. no act is right or wrong in itself
    III. the principle of utility need *not* be applied in every situation
    IV. the principle of utility needs to be applied in every situation
    V. past experience is not a reliable guide for judging actions
    The CORRECT combination is:

    A. I, IV, V   B. II, IV, V   C. I, III, V   D. IV, V   E. I, II

50. Rule-utilitarianism states that
    I. moral principles should encompass typical actions that people perform frequently
    II. deciding the moral rightness of each act is inefficient and does not promote happiness
    III. sometimes an action ought to be performed, morally speaking, even though it does not promote the greatest happiness
    IV. no action should be performed if it itself does not increase the happiness of everyone
    V. past experiences are no basis for moral judgment

    The CORRECT combination is:

    A. II, III, IV   B. I, II, III   C. I, III, V   D. II, IV, V   E. I, II

KEY (CORRECT ANSWERS)

1. E	11. D	21. D	31. D	41. D
2. E	12. B	22. C	32. D	42. D
3. D	13. C	23. C	33. D	43. E
4. E	14. B	24. D	34. C	44. A
5. E	15. E	25. E	35. A	45. A
6. D	16. C	26. A	36. E	46. C
7. A	17. E	27. B	37. E	47. C
8. C	18. E	28. B	38. E	48. A
9. B	19. A	29. B	39. D	49. B
10. E	20. A	30. D	40. D	50. B

www.ingramcontent.com/pod-product-compliance
Lightning Source LLC
Chambersburg PA
CBHW082040300426
44117CB00015B/2553